Running with Asthma: An
Asthmatic Runner's Memoir

Running with Asthma: An Asthmatic Runner's Memoir

John Terry McConnell

To Marla, who turned on the light to get me out of the darkness

ISBN: 1512151645
ISBN 13: 9781512151640
Library of Congress Control Number: 2015907798
CreateSpace Independent Publishing Platform
North Charleston, South Carolina

Acknowledgments

Special thanks to Marla McConnell who encouraged me to write this book.

Special thanks go to the greatest of all distance-running coaches, the late Kermit Ambrose, Birmingham Seaholm High School, Birmingham, Michigan.

Thanks go to the people who provided insight for me as I wrote this book: Linda Kahn, Dr. Richard Parmett, Dr. Richard Warner, Dr. Robert Ajello, Dr. Jim Lemkin, Bruce Bennett, Karin Purugganan, Melissa McConnell, Matt McConnell, Jason Reisch, Bill Ivey, Dan Millman. and, Lee Evers.

The graphic on the cover of this book is from 123RF

This book is intended to provide a story of what worked for the author. The reader should not infer or conclude the results of the author will be the same for you. You must consult your physician prior to engaging in any exercise activity or changing of diet. The author nor the publisher assumes any liability whatsoever associated with any claims resulting from a decision on your part to engage in exercise activity or changes in diet. If you are unwilling to accept this disclaimer, you should return the book for a full refund. Contact the author at: runnerwithasthma@gmail.com

Contents

Prologue

In 1953, I was six years old. My family lived in an apartment at 624 Custer Street in Evanston, Illinois, about two hundred yards from the L train that led to nearby Chicago. Looking out our second-floor living room window, you'd see the National Biscuit Company Building, the L tracks, and the IGA food market. Looking back into the living room you'd see a model gas station and toy cars spread across the living room floor. I pushed plenty of toy cars up and down that gas station's ramp. It was a great place to play, except for one thing. The apartment was often full of cigarette smoke. It got hard to breathe. And 1953 was the year I was diagnosed with asthma.

In that same year, I saw something profoundly beautiful. In our living room, there was a black-and-white television, an eighteen-inch model. Color TV was not available yet. Chicago Cubs baseball games were on WGN almost every day from April to September. I spent many hours watching my favorite Cubs in action, especially Ernie Banks, the Cubs' shortstop. One day, my dad took me to see a Cubs game. We boarded the nearby L train that took us to Wrigley Field, pushed through the turnstiles, and found our seats. That's when I saw it! The Cubs' baseball field had bright-green, sparkling grass. The outfield walls were covered with verdant-green ivy. Wrigley Field was not the dull gray field of our black-and-white television. Wrigley Field was beautiful. The Cubs' uniforms weren't dull gray, either. The royal-blue hats with a red C on them, the royal-blue pinstripes on the brilliant white shirts and pants, the red-white-and-blue Cubs insignia on the left front of the jersey. Beautiful. Watching the Pirates play the Cubs that day was like being in the Land of Oz.

As a six-year-old, I learned to love sports. Each morning when the *Chicago Tribune* landed at our door, it was the sports page, not the funny papers, that caught my attention. My favorite time was spent throwing or catching baseballs. In our family, the love of sports was almost sacred. My grandfather founded the first professional football team in Minnesota around 1900. My dad was an excellent golfer, and my mother was a superb tennis player. Sports for me, then, wasn't just a part of life; it was life itself, and a blessing.

But, for me, sports turned out to be a kind of curse as well. I couldn't keep up with the other kids on the playing field. While playing basketball, there'd be special time-outs called just for me so I could catch my breath. It's tough to play sports when it's almost impossible to keep running. That's what asthma does. Worse yet, it hurt not being able to run like the other kids. It made me feel like some kind of limited human being. I wanted to be unlimited.

I

Growing Up Limited

In late summer of 1955, we moved from Evanston to Birmingham, Michigan, a suburb of Detroit. My asthma immediately got worse, and for a few months, playing sports was no longer an option. Every Saturday morning, my parents drove me from our home in Birmingham to Henry Ford Hospital in Detroit. We went up the elevator to the asthma and allergy department to see the doctor. He had a white coat, black hair, and a black stethoscope around his neck. On the white walls of his office, there was a large drawing of the human body, and an illustration of a pair of lungs.

The doctor told me, "Asthma happens in the bronchi of the lungs, the small and midsize breathing tubes."

"Why do I have asthma?" I asked.

The doctor continued. "Different things trigger asthma. Things like dust, mold, stress, house dust mites, cigarette smoke, air pollution, animal hair, cold air, colds, flu, pollen, and exercise."

"That's a lot."

"All these things make muscles around the airways tight," the doctor continued. "The airways swell and become inflamed. The inflamed lung tissues produce extra mucus."

"What's mucus?"

"It's this goo in your lungs. Understand?" the doctor asked.

"Yes."

He continued. "Breathing is hard because the airways narrow. There's too much goo. Less air comes in. Do you know what happens next?"

"Yeah, with all the goo in my lungs, breathing's hard."

"Right," the doctor said. "When the airways narrow and there's a lot of goo, what happens to the air you breathe?"

"There's less of it?"

"Yes," the doctor continued. "Especially, less oxygen. The blood needs the oxygen to carry nutrients all over your body."

"What are nutrients?"

"That's the food your muscles need to make you move," the doctor said. "When your muscles don't get enough food, what happens?"

"They move slower?"

"That's right," the doctor said.

"So I move slower, too?"

"Yes."

The doctor left the room. Soon a nurse came in with a rack of about twenty needles. She gave me ten shots in each arm to test for allergies. About 70 percent of all asthmatics have allergies, me included. Mine were grass, trees, pollen, mold, house dust, and tobacco smoke. Both my arms were really sore from the shots. Between the drive to and from Detroit, the consultation with the doctor, and the shots from the nurse, it seemed like it took up most of Saturday. I needed to get an allergy shot every Saturday, so the drive between Birmingham and Henry Ford Hospital became very familiar. That fall, Saturday was not a day to look forward to.

After all that trouble, it just got a lot harder to breathe. In the fall of 1955, the mucus in my lungs was constant. I was sick and missed a month of school. Upon returning to my third-grade classroom, my attention wavered and a lot of my time was spent looking out the window. Not breathing well left me in a fog—another aspect of being limited, another side effect of asthma.

By eighth grade, I found that running slowly around the school gym once was my limit. Running forced me to spit up a lot of mucus. That was unpleasant, not only for me but also for others to witness. Having to spit up all that mucus made me feel weird, different. Not breathing well resulted in my lack of stamina and physical strength. I became a target for typical eighth-grade harassment from bigger, stronger guys, especially from one big, strong eighth-grader named Tom. After months of daily insults from Tom, I challenged him to a wrestling match in gym class. We wrestled for the entire period, and he pinned me on the mat at least twenty times. At the end of gym class, I was full of bruises, exhausted, and the daily harassment continued. Yet, to this day, that wrestling match is one of the proudest moments of my life. For the entire gym class, I never gave up.

To my knowledge, no one else at school or in the neighborhood had asthma. The prevalence of asthma in the wider world was unknown to me then. It would have surprised me to know that by 2014, 8 percent of all Americans and 10 percent of American children would have asthma, that the percentage of Americans with asthma would continue to grow, and that, worldwide, 250,000 people a year would die from asthma. Having no idea about this, I felt very alone with my breathing problem.

My doctor advised me to not go on Cub Scout or Boy Scout overnight camping trips. The cold air would be bad for my lungs.

It was difficult for me to compete in sports. I got cut from sports teams on a regular basis. I even got cut from the school glee club.

The sense of being limited grew inside me. It was like I was wearing a T-shirt with the word "limited" on the front. Being healthy and good at sports became my standard for evaluating people. By that standard, I fell very short. That T-shirt seemed impossible to take off. It made me quite uncomfortable in my own skin.

II

I Get By with a Little Help from My Inhaler

In the summer of 1962, I spent four weeks at the Thunderbird Sports Camp in Baldwin, Michigan, two hundred miles northwest of my home near Detroit. My plan was to get in shape for junior varsity football. Prior to my leaving for Thunderbird, my doctor handed me my first inhaler.

"What will this thing do for me?"

"It will relax the muscles around your lungs," Dr. Burger said. "So you'll breathe easier when you play sports."

What Dr. Burger gave me was an albuterol sulfate bronchodilator inhaler. It made it easier to breathe while running. It's called a quick-relief inhaler. It should be taken fifteen minutes before exercise, and the dose lasts four to six hours. The type of drug used in it is called a beta2-agonist. (The brand of quick-relief inhaler I use now is called ProAir.)

At Thunderbird, this inhaler worked wonders for me. We did distance running as a camp activity. In a mile race through the woods, I finished ninth out of fifteen runners. For me that was a real victory. For once, the worst player on the field wasn't me. Running helped to clear my chest congestion, and after a run, breathing was easier.

A coach at Thunderbird, Kermit Ambrose, used to tell us stories about track and cross-country. Ambrose would often say, "With hard work, you can succeed in sports." He'd show home movies about his cross-country and track teams at Birmingham Seaholm High School. His teams were very successful.

Somewhere in the back of my mind it registered. *I could do this. I could be determined to succeed as a runner.*

In the fall of 1962, a new policy was set in our house. No smoking was allowed. People had to smoke outside. I played junior varsity football at Birmingham Seaholm High School that fall without much success. Blocking and tackling was not my thing. Coach Ambrose encouraged me to go out for track in the spring. Fortunately, Ambrose didn't cut anybody. I ran a 58.9 second quarter-mile that season. A combination of my inhaler, Ambrose's workouts, and the no-smoking policy in our house enabled me to run without much congestion.

I also played on a Colt League baseball team that spring. Our team won the league championship. My 0.186 batting average didn't place me among the team's star players. But in the league championship game, my sacrifice grounder scored the winning run. At a dinner at Orchard Lake Country Club, all the players received trophies. After the trophy presentation, in walked Gordie Howe of the Detroit Red Wings, one of the best ice hockey players of all time.

In his speech to us, Howe said, "If you're playing tennis with some guy ten years from now, and he beats you, don't shake his hand. Instead, look him in the eye and say, 'Next time, I'm going to beat you.'"

What in the world did Gordie Howe mean by that? My chances of winning at tennis were usually slim to none. If I followed Howe's suggestion, I'd look like a fool.

III

The Universe Opens Up

In the movie *Field of Dreams*, the character Ray Kinsella, played by Kevin Costner, is talking to the fictional author Terence Mann, played by James Earl Jones. Kinsella recites a quote from Mann's writing, something like this: "Sometimes, the universe opens up and shows you what can happen." In the last two years of high school, my universe actually did open up.

In the summer before my junior year, my aunt told me not to drink milk and to stay away from all dairy products. I did as she instructed, and as a result, my asthma got better. That fall, I ran junior varsity cross-country and was able to run the two-mile course in under thirteen minutes. Our team won the state championship that season.

At the end of our junior year, my friend on the cross-country team, Mike Johnstone, said to our group of runners, "We need to step up to the next level. All of the best runners have graduated or moved away."

"I'm up for that. Sounds cool," I said.

"Yeah, me, too," said my running buddy, Bob Zane.

In the summer of 1964, my friends Dick Walker, Johnstone, Zane, and I trained every evening at North Hills Golf Course across the street from Oakland Hills Country Club. With the help of my inhaler, no dairy products, and no secondhand smoke, my running improved enough to keep up with those guys. We didn't know anything about hard/easy training or rest days. We went out to North Hills every evening and ran our butts off. We ran in a pack. Fast up the hill, then a recovery jog, and fast up the hill again. Sometimes we'd run in a single-file line, and the runner in the back would sprint up to the front and take the lead. We'd keep this up until someone called it quits, and then we'd jog back to Walker's red Chevrolet Corvair for the ride home, exhausted but happy. That summer taught us all the value of determination in all our endeavors. When school started again, we'd all be first-rate distance runners.

In August, the four of us ran in a mile race on the track at what is now the Cranbrook Kingswood Upper School. One of the runners on the track that day was a six-foot-six guy who lived a block away from me and had also been coached by Ambrose at Seaholm High School. He was Jack Bacheler, who was then running in college at Miami of Ohio. Bacheler went on to compete in the 1968 and 1972 Olympics, finishing ninth in the marathon that the American Frank Shorter won in 1972.

Johnstone was a captain on our cross-country team. He was a natural leader. One day at practice, before the workout began, we were all sitting in the locker room, surrounded by big gray lockers and wooden benches. Johnstone and a few of his teammates stood up and began singing a song made up by another team member, Tom Tollefson, to the tune of "Come a Little Bit Closer" by Jay and the Americans. They sang, "Run a little bit faster. The pace is too slow. Run a little bit faster. You're almost done and there's not far to go."

That hard-working, good-singing team ended up fourth in the state, and it felt great to be part of that talented group. At the end of my senior year, I was running the mile in 5:00 and the half-mile in 2:10.

Coach Ambrose would often tell all of his runners, "You have no idea how good a runner you could be." I was beginning to believe him. Ambrose had another saying that he must have repeated a million times to his runners, "When the going gets tough, the tough get going."

By the end of my senior year of high school, my asthma virtually disappeared. Running became a way of redefining myself. Being a varsity runner on the school cross-country and track teams made me feel good about myself. So what if I wasn't that good at baseball, tennis, or golf? I found my niche: distance running. My sense of being limited began to fade. Running in high school under Coach Ambrose taught me the value of determination. Determination was now ingrained in my psyche. Determination would drive me when I applied it and haunt me when I ignored it.

IV

Running Goes South

About 350 miles south of Birmingham, Michigan, was my college, DePauw University, in Greencastle, Indiana. I ran on the JV track and cross-country teams during my freshman year, but my heart wasn't in it. When our team traveled to Terre Haute, Indiana, for a meet against Indiana State, I learned a hard lesson about asthma management. My albuterol sulfate inhaler ran out of medicine, and I had no back-up inhaler. I had to drop out of the race. By the end of my freshman year, my running had ceased. My freshman year was a step backward. Whatever I did, whether it was going out on dates, studying, or taking exams, seemed to turn out weird. It got harder to breathe, too. That T-shirt with the word "limited" on it started to feel tighter, especially when comparing myself to the other athletes around the campus.

In the summer before my sophomore year, my attitude changed. I trained hard all summer in preparation for cross-country season. My asthma was almost nonexistent. My friend Bob Zane had become a standout distance runner at Adrian College. I figured I could do the same at DePauw. Taking my albuterol sulfate inhaler before a run was my only asthma treatment. After running about twenty-five miles a week all summer, the coach had us running fifty miles a week. In early September 1966, there was a four-mile cross-country race just outside of Greencastle. The course was on a tree-lined dirt road that ran alongside Big Walnut Creek to the covered bridge and back. I was running neck and neck with Dan Spears, the number-one runner on our team. Dan sprinted ahead of me twenty yards from the finish line. That was OK. We were both way ahead of the competition, and matching Spears stride for stride for almost four miles was no small achievement. The next race would be against our biggest rival, Wabash College.

The night before the race, I went to see a movie: *Who's Afraid of Virginia Woolf?* That movie is full of conflict between a married couple, and it triggered an inner conflict about expectations others had for me. My stepmother had one agenda for me regarding my religion. My father had another agenda for me regarding being in a fraternity. My own agenda was limited to wanting to please others instead of communicating in a forthright, honest way about my own needs. Telling people my true feelings wasn't in my game plan. All my unexpressed feelings, plus the fact that I'd been running way too much for the past two weeks, coalesced into a kind of asthma volcano erupting inside me.

On the trip to Crawfordsville, Indiana for the Wabash race, my body didn't feel right. As the starting gun went off in front of a red brick Wabash dormitory, my stomach felt queasy. Two hundred yards into the race, there was nothing in my tank. I could barely jog. It was hard to breathe. It was an asthma attack.

For the next week, I was flat on my back at the college infirmary with pneumonia.

When I returned to the team a month later, the coach said, "Tough break, Terry. You ran well before you got sick."

"Yeah," I said. "But not now."

All my conditioning was gone. It was a struggle just to run a lap around the track. Very discouraging. The aftereffects of the asthma attack rendered me useless as a distance runner for the entire season. I lacked the energy to run and my chest stayed full of congestion for a month. All that running last summer for nothing. Could asthma take away my one athletic talent? It sure as hell seemed like it could.

That was the end of competitive running for me in college. My running, most definitely, went south.

V

A War between Greek Gods

After my sophomore year of college, playing tennis once in a while replaced distance running. Something huge was now missing in my life. Running had become a way to overcome my limits, a way to affirm all my possibilities. I'd gone from an eighth grader who could barely run around the gym to a young man who could run a mile in five minutes flat. Running had fortified my spirit and enabled me to believe in myself. Getting pneumonia made me think running was no good for me so I decided to quit running. What a stupid decision. It was like having a gold coin in my pocket and throwing it away.

After college, I became a middle-school social studies teacher while getting a master's degree in education. It was a stressful job, quite a challenge to teach American history to over a hundred rambunctious eighth graders every day. My lungs and my health didn't seem too important to me then. I started using tobacco. Not a lot, but enough to do me harm. Smoking cigarettes made my asthma worse.

My asthma got out of control sometimes. In graduate school in 1972, pneumonia smacked me for the second time and laid me up for a couple of weeks. I sensed something was missing in my life. "What was it?" I asked myself. As the 70s unfolded I began to realize what was missing was the determination Coach Ambrose had taught me in high school.

In 1979, I turned to running to try to recover that determination. By 1983, my running became a top priority. Most days found me running at least three or four miles. Yet I hadn't totally given up smoking. Sometimes I'd go a few months without it, but smoking haunted me. My life was like a war between the Greek gods Apollo and Dionysus. To me, these mythological gods symbolized urges going on inside me. Inside my head, Apollo urged me to train hard and strive for a personal record during each race. In Greek mythology, Apollo actually was the god of physical training and healing. Dionysus, in Greek mythology, was the god of wine, fertility, wild partying, and doing whatever felt good. On another side of my brain, Dionysus prodded me to do what felt good, which for me was smoking cigarettes. The battle raged every time I went by a 7-Eleven store. Apollo and Dionysus battled daily. I threw away more cigarettes than I ever smoked.

My asthma became unpredictable. Some days, I could only breathe well enough to jog. On other days, I had no breathing problems at all and did the fastest running of my life. My lungs were a case of Dr. Jekyll and Mr. Hyde. On a given day, it was hard to know which pair of lungs would show up. In 1984, after not smoking at all for seven months, I ran my best 10K race ever in 38:50 on a very flat course at Hains Point next to the Potomac River in Washington, DC. To this day, that personal record is like a rock, an achievement at the core of my being.

This was a very rough time for me emotionally. I was going through a divorce and my stress level was high. Running was there for me. It was a way of coping with stress and feeling good about myself. Coaching track and cross-country at the high school where I worked helped my running and my self-esteem. It was fun to try to keep up with the runners on my team as we covered miles.

In the winter of 1985, my doctor gave me a prescription for the Azmacort inhaler. This drug was a corticosteroid, to be taken along with my albuterol sulfate beta2-agonist. Unlike albuterol, the

Azmacort was not for quick relief. Instead, the purpose was to relieve asthma symptoms over a long period of time. It worked well, and my asthma symptoms lessened. Later I would switch from Azmacort to another corticosteroid, Advair Diskus.

In the spring of 1985, I ran my first and last marathon, in Washington, DC. My breathing was now consistently excellent and so was my running. I hadn't smoked at all in a year. This marathon provided a very interesting course that ran through all the districts of Washington, DC. Running at a pace for a three hour (3:00) marathon, at the twenty-mile mark the ball of my left foot just gave out. I hobbled the last six miles and ended up running the marathon in about four-and-a-half hours. That experience broke my motivation to run competitively. It would be my last race for twenty-two years. The final six miles of what had almost been an awesome marathon run felt like a thousand miles.

VI

Why Is My Asthma Gettin' Worse?

Things went downhill after the marathon. In 1986, Billy Ocean had a top forty hit record with the song, "When the Going Gets Tough, the Tough Get Going." That song haunted me. Every time I heard it, I thought about running under Coach Ambrose in high school. The title of that song was exactly what Ambrose used to tell us. The song reminded me how much I missed running and the determination that running brought out in me. My biggest achievement was in 1989 when I quit smoking totally. No backsliding since then, not even once.

One would think totally quitting smoking would make my asthma better, but in the 1990s, my asthma got worse. I was now in my forties. Running fast for distance became impossible. My lot was more pneumonia, frequent nebulizer treatments, and constant congestion. Two glasses of champagne at a wedding in 1993 put me in the emergency room with an asthma attack. After that trip to the emergency room, beer and wine went on my "can't do" list. The mold in those drinks made my asthma worse. The next year, after a pizza party, I could barely breathe. As with beer and wine, pizza and cheese had to go.

In 1994, my son's soccer team sponsored a parents' soccer game. It was a bright October Saturday afternoon, a perfect day for athletic activity. The parents, both men and women, were having a great time kicking the ball around the field. Playing in that game in my mid forties, my asthma was so bad, after five minutes I had to quit. I couldn't catch my breath while running after the ball. That was one awful experience, worse than trying to run around the gym in the eighth grade. I felt totally limited on that soccer field, as if my inner strength was seeping right out of me. It felt horrible to not be able to run around a soccer field.

Running now made my asthma worse. When I tried to resume running, a run of three miles resulted in time off of work because of illness. Looking back at those years, I wasn't managing my asthma very well. Managing stress was a real problem. As head librarian of a high school, it was my job to manage a lot of people—staff, students, and volunteers. Problems at work increased my stress level. Reflecting back on those problems, my communication skills needed some work.

My asthma got so bad I went to my personal physician for advice. He said that I needed frequent nebulizer treatments and wrote me a prescription for a nebulizer and the drug albuterol. I bought my own nebulizer to get the treatments at home. A nebulizer is an electronic device that is either battery operated or plugged into an AC outlet. It turns medication into a mist that is breathed into the lungs via a tube held in the mouth. At one point in the nineties, I used my nebulizer every day for a month. To use the nebulizer, I mixed a dose of albuterol with a saline solution. It was quite discouraging for me to have to rely on a nebulizer in order to ease chest congestion. When I look back at that stage of my life, my high stress level coincided with my increased asthma symptoms.

When my asthma improved a little, I asked my doctor about continuing to run. He said my running career was over. The thought of that made me sad and discouraged. My old high school running buddy, Mike Johnstone, invited me to a reunion of runners back in Birmingham, Michigan. The runners from the class of 1965 were going to run a mile race about thirty years after high school. The race would be on our old high school track.

I had to decline the invitation. I couldn't even run a mile. It seemed like that T-shirt with "limited" on the front would never come off my chest.

VII

The Universe Shifts

Limited! That was getting to be a real drag. Reading self-help books became a habit for me. My favorite self-help author was Dan Millman, who wrote *The Way of the Peaceful Warrior*. In August 2005, at a weekend workshop at the Omega Institute in Rhinebeck, New York, I met Millman and learned about the Peaceful Warrior Workout.

Millman demonstrated the workout and conducted many activities designed to develop self-confidence. A lot of what he taught was positive thinking. He had many techniques designed to help people believe in their ability to achieve their goals. The culminating activity was to break a wooden board placed between two cinder blocks with a blow from the hand. There were probably fifty people at Millman's seminar, men and women ranging in age from their twenties to their eighties. Amazingly, almost everyone was able to break their board, including me. That weekend, I stayed at the Super 8 Motel in Kingston, near Rhinebeck. After the amazing experience with Millman on Saturday, I returned to my motel room (room 232) at about 9:00 p.m., left the room, locked the door, went out, bought a submarine sandwich, came back, went out again, and locked the door. Upon my return the submarine sandwich was gone! So was my watch! There was a book sitting on the desk in room 232 titled *Mysteries of Science*. How did *that* get there? Where were my watch and sandwich? Those were my angry questions for the hotel manager. He said he'd look into it, so I gave him my address. A week later my watch was returned to me in the mail. It was the weirdest experience of my life. Why would anyone steal my submarine sandwich and my watch and then arrange to send my watch back to me a week later? A thief would have just taken both. That book, *Mysteries of Science*, has a chapter on parallel universes. It was kind of like my universe shifted that weekend from one parallel universe to another.

I really don't know much about parallel universes, but, come to think of it, my universe made a huge shift that weekend. Millman's deep-breathing exercises improved my asthma a great deal. Doing the Peaceful Warrior Workout was a real turning point for me in my lifelong battle with asthma. In my fifties, I could feel the mucus clogging the lower portion of my lungs every day. It seemed there was no way to get rid of it. Running was now not an option to relieve that congestion. However, doing the Peaceful Warrior Workout improved my breathing, and my asthma symptoms diminished. These exercises were done with slow, deep breaths through the nose. This deep breathing expanded my lung capacity and made the muscles in my diaphragm stronger. I'd been breathing through my mouth my whole life. Breathing through the nose was a new experience. These exercises took just four minutes a day. If I woke up in the middle of the night with chest congestion, doing the Peaceful Warrior Workout lessened my congestion considerably. Instructions on the Peaceful Warrior website, http://www.PeacefulWarrior.com, can show someone how to do these exercises correctly. At this website, Millman offers a course on how to do the Peaceful Warrior Workout for as little as one dollar. I'd advise anyone with asthma to consult with their personal physician before beginning the Peaceful Warrior Workout or any deep-breathing exercise.

The Peaceful Warrior Workout should only be done for four or five minutes, as Dan Millman specifies. I got carried away with this workout, doing one section of it, the stationary cross-country ski exercise regularly for forty-five minutes. This may have contributed to a knee injury. When I kept this workout to four or five minutes, it worked wonders for me.

The Peaceful Warrior Workout helped me focus on breathing correctly. There were other breathing exercises I learned as well. I'd lie down on the floor with my right hand on my sternum and my left hand on my lower abdomen. When breathing correctly, my left hand would go up on the inhale and down on the exhale. My right hand would not move at all. The inhale took four counts and the exhale took eight counts. The inhale was done with less effort while the exhale was done with more. In the exhale, my goal was to pull my belly button toward my spine. I practiced this type of breathing every day while walking.

Deep breathing expanded my lung capacity, increased my blood flow to my brain, and lessened my lung inflammation. Like me, most asthmatics have shallow breathing patterns. Nose breathing helped me to change that, to get the air deeper in my lungs.

The Peaceful Warrior Workout improved my breathing, but running in the polluted air of the DC area was not an option. I was happy just breathing better.

VIII

New Town, New Lungs

In 2005, I moved north from Washington, DC, to a rural mountainous area.

It was like magic. My asthma improved immediately for the following reasons:

1. Less air pollution. Living in a mountainous area away from huge amounts of auto traffic and industrial air pollution provided me a safe haven from air pollution that tends to collect in valleys such as the river valley in the DC area.
2. More trees. A study at Columbia University showed that in New York City, the more trees on the block, the less incidence of childhood asthma. On the mountain where my new home was, trees were everywhere.
3. No animal dander. There was no cat in my new home, so animal dander was no longer a problem.
4. No mold. In my new mountain home, the basement and the attic were treated to get rid of mold. Mold can lead to serious asthma problems.
5. No dust. My house in the mountains was kept free of dust. Dust is an asthma trigger. The type of heat I chose for my house was an important decision. Clean-burning gas heat was not an option, so oil heat was my choice. Wood stoves are

popular in my area, but these stoves put a lot of particles in the air inside the house. Not good for breathing. The fan for my oil furnace was set to run frequently to improve indoor air quality. It turns out that the correct furnace filter is an important consideration for a home with a furnace. A disposable furnace filter should be used. It's important to change the furnace filter once a month during heating season. The filter should be corrugated to enhance airflow. Flanders NaturalAire furnace filters work well for me. It's smart to avoid metal furnace filters that are washed and reused. They do not trap enough dust, so more dust circulates in the house (Bob LaCoy, heating and cooling specialist, in discussion with the author, August 6, 2014).

6. In my new home there were mainly uncovered wood floors and not much carpeting. Carpets can hold asthma triggers such as pollen, animal dander and dust.

For all these reasons, my breathing improved.

After settling into my new home, it was time to consult with my new physician, Richard Warner, MD. I told him about my hope to run again. Warner didn't reject the idea of my running again, as my doctor in the DC area had. Warner spent time listening to me. He knew a lot about the body and health, and he happily shared what he knew. What a pleasant surprise to find a doctor like this. My experience with an HMO in the DC area was much more impersonal. Doctors there didn't seem to have much time to consult with me regarding my asthma. Being a competitive bicyclist himself and only a couple of years younger than me, Warner empathized with my desire to compete again as a runner. Warner referred me to Robert Ajello, MD, a pulmonary specialist.

Ajello examined me and told me it would be OK for me to run again, even ramp it up if I wanted to. Not just an occasional jog, but serious running. He told me that many Olympic athletes have asthma.

I was shocked by what Ajello told me. Being skeptical, I did a lot of Google searches using terms like "Olympic distance runners" and "asthma" ("Asthma All-Stars," *Breathe Easy Play Hard Foundation*, 2015. Last modified Feb. 4, 2015. http://www.breatheeasyplayhard.com/pg/jsp/general/asthmaallstars.jsp#olympic). The list of Olympic runners with asthma is impressive: Jim Ryun (set a world record in the mile run), Mary Decker Slaney (held every American record for women's running from the eight hundred-meter run to the ten thousand-meter run), Alberto Salazar (winner of the New York Marathon 1980, 1981, 1982; Boston Marathon 1982), Jackie Joyner-Kersee (winner of the Olympic Heptathlon 1988, 1992), Paula Radcliffe (world-record holder in the women's marathon), Haile Gebrselassie (held twenty-six distance-running world records), and Galen Rupp (silver medal in the 2012 Olympics ten-thousand-meter run and an American record in the ten-thousand-meter run).

With my doctors' approval and my knowledge of the great distance runners with asthma, my running program resumed at the age of fifty-nine. Now I had a shot at taking back something that had been lost: Running for distance. Running strong. Running fast. Running with the determination I'd learned from Coach Ambrose in high school. The T-shirt with the word "limited" on it began to feel loose on my chest. Maybe I could take it off.

IX

On the Run Again

My running program began in the spring of 2006. I'd been doing the Peaceful Warrior Workout for about eight months, and the breathing exercises in this workout had significantly improved my breathing. As a precaution, my albuterol inhaler was in my pocket during a run. I've never needed it, but Jim Ryun did. He had a severe asthma attack with difficulty breathing. Fortunately he had his inhaler. It provided him quick relief after the fifteen hundred-meter run at the 1968 Olympics in Mexico City. If it could happen to him, it could happen to me. When an asthma attack occurs while running, it's wise to take multiple puffs of albuterol to stop the attack. If the albuterol causes the body to shake, it's time to stop taking it. Also, my cell phone was nearby just in case I needed to make a 911 call during a run. Fortunately, that's not happened yet. It's smart to be aware of the signs of an asthma attack: wheezing, breathing more quickly than usual, breathing with more effort, and flaring nostrils.

I took my first run in March 2006. It was only half a mile, but it was tough to make it two times around the track. After a few months of running, I began to feel a lot stronger. The usual two or three miles didn't seem like enough. So my next run was six miles long. Talk about soreness after a run! Thank God for the massage therapist who eased the pain of my lower-back muscles. She also told me to take a few days off from running. To increase weekly running mileage, it's best to increase no more than 5 percent a week. After that sore experience, my longest runs were never more than four to five miles. I ran slowly. Running fast would have been hard on my lungs and made me sick. During a slow run, it is possible to carry on a conversation with someone. During a fast run, that's impossible. Even running slowly, I experienced a lot of congestion and had to spit into my handkerchief often.

There are benefits to breathing through the nose while running. Breathing through the nose gets more air into the chest. It also moistens, warms, and filters the air better than breathing through the mouth. Warm, moist air is the best air for optimal breathing (Bruce Bennett, physician assistant, in discussion with the author, November 11, 2013). The problem is, like many asthmatics, I'd been breathing through my mouth my whole life! Learning to breathe through the nose took some getting used to. On my first attempt, I stopped after twenty yards, thinking, *This is impossible!* After repeated attempts, it got easier. However, it was only possible for me to breathe through the nose when running slowly. Running fast called for mouth breathing. Whether one is doing nose or mouth breathing, the focus is more on the exhale than the inhale.

Because dehydration can cause congestion, I'd drink a lot of water before each run. After each run, Gatorade was my drink of choice since it restores lost electrolytes. Later, Smartwater became my after-running drink. Smartwater has electrolytes and no sugar.

To keep my lungs decongested, I needed to do the Peaceful Warrior Workout every day, usually in the morning before work. This workout is not meant to be strenuous the way a distance run is. There's not much sweating involved. That's quite different from the end of a distance run, where my T-shirt is drenched in sweat.

Most of my runs took place in the afternoon, during lunch or after work. On weekends I tried to run in the mornings. That's usually the best time to run for asthmatics. In the spring and summer, it was important to know the pollen count before each run. This can be done by going to Pollen.com. If the pollen count was really high, I could run indoors on a treadmill at the YMCA that day.

Running in different locations was a problem. When I went back to the DC area to visit relatives, my asthma would get worse when running outside. The solution was to only run indoors, at the indoor track at the local YMCA. On trips to other cities, the results varied. Running outdoors in Los Angeles, I got so sick I needed to see a doctor immediately. LA is like a big bowl created by nearby mountains. The air pollution can't escape the city. It was easier for me to run outdoors in Chicago. It's flat there, and the breeze from Lake Michigan blows some of the polluted air away. (A good web source to check for air quality is the Environmental Protection Agency's web site, http://airnow.gov/. Select "Air Quality Index," type in your zip code and click on "Go.")

I didn't have to travel far to encounter air pollution. I spent one evening at the house of friends who smoked cigarettes. It was hard to breathe even though they smoked outside. Enough smoke filtered back in the house that the next day I could barely breathe when running. It took a few days for my breathing to return to normal.

When I started to run again in my new, rural, mountainous home, it was necessary to relearn the technique of running. It was vital to learn to relax my body and use proper running form. Learning to run is a lot like learning to hit a baseball. Good hitters practice their swing thousands of times. A good hitter swings the same way with each practice swing. A good runner uses the same running form with each stride. The purpose of running form is to move the body along the ground as efficiently as possible. There should be no wasted effort. This is true for all runners and especially true when running with asthma. I need all the energy I can get! There is none to waste. Numerous websites can be accessed to view good running form. You can find a great example of this at http://www.runnersworld.com/getting-started/the-starting-line-proper-running-form.

At this website, click on "Good Running Form." Some of the key elements of good running form are as follows: back straight but not stiff, arms moving forward and backward (not side to side), and hands relaxed. Lightly touch the thumb with the forefinger on each hand. Don't make a fist. Keep the shoulders low, and don't slump them. Look straight ahead. Hold the head even so it does not bob up and down much. Land flatfooted and make sure each foot does not point in or out. Keep the feet pointed straight ahead to help prevent leg and foot injuries. Don't push off from the toes. The push comes from the hamstring and core muscles. To increase speed, lean forward slightly from the ankles while keeping the back straight. Land the feet on the ground as lightly as possible.

The most important aspect of running form for me to follow is to keep my back straight, relaxed, and leaning slightly forward. *If my back isn't straight, air can't get into my lungs efficiently.* Any exercise that improves posture improves air exchange in the lungs. In a healthy lung, the breathing tubes themselves are more straight, less crooked ("Asthma," *Paediatric Society of New Zealand and Starship Foundation.* Last modified 2013. http://www.kidshealth.org.nz/asthma).

When walking after a run, I keep practicing some of these principles: back straight and relaxed, and feet landing lightly, flat, and pointed straight ahead. Like baseball hitters' swings, each runner's form is a little different. Running form should feel comfortable. With a few months of running under my belt and a running form that was right for me, it was time for some serious, competitive running.

X

Running 3K Races

In August 2007, I entered my first race, a 3K, which is 1.86 miles. I'd advise anyone with asthma to consult with their personal physician before attempting a race. A race is likely to put much more strain on the body than a jog around the park.

At the starting gun, I felt apprehensive. Would a sixty-year-old man be able to race again as he did as a teenager and as a man in his thirties? Would my body allow me to run fast?

Bang! The race started and I went out fast, trying to keep up with a variety of runners from preteens up to runners even older than me. I maintained a fast pace (for me) during the first mile and didn't slow down much going up a hill. In the second mile, I had enough energy to continue at the same pace. At the finish line, with an enthusiastic crowd cheering me on, my time was 14:27. My run on that hilly course had gone well. Two years earlier, there was no way I could have done that. Running fast—fast for me, that is—left me with the pleasant buzz in my head that people call a runner's high.

My health improved so much that my personal physician, Dr. Warner, suggested that I get off some of my medications. There were four: (1) ProAir (albuterol sulfate inhaler), two puffs in the morning and two at night; (2) Advair Diskus 250/50, one puff in the morning, one puff at night; (3) Montelukast (Singulair), 10 mg, one pill at night; and (4) Theophylline, four tablets of 200 mg a day. In 2007, my dosage of ProAir was cut to two puffs and only before a run. I stopped taking Theophylline in the fall of 2009 and immediately got a bad chest cold. My second effort in the spring of 2012 was successful because I did the tapering off gradually. For a month, only three pills a day, the next month only two, the next month one, and the month after that, none. In 2013, I successfully cut my dose of Advair from morning and night to only night.

As a person with lifelong asthma, I was well aware of the sickening feeling of the mucus in my lungs and the foul taste of the mucus in my mouth as I spit it out. Slowly, between 2007 and 2013, that sickening feeling and foul taste began to fade. Instead of making my asthma worse, running was now making my asthma better.

Drinking a hot cup of coffee before a run was an effective way to lessen congestion during a run. As the coffee went down, my chest seemed to loosen up.

When I moved to my new mountain home, I went to work as a high school librarian. The library was almost always crowded, and it was my job to keep the noise down and get the students on task with their studies. Going running on my lunch break made it easier to deal with the students and their problems more effectively for the rest of the school day. The word "limited" was beginning to fade on the T-shirt I'd worn since childhood.

Some of the students who came into the library were ice hockey players. It was fun to tell them my Gordie Howe story, where Howe said, "If a guy beats you at tennis, don't shake his hand. Say, 'Next time, I'll beat you.'" I didn't understand the meaning of Howe's words for me, but something about these words stuck with me fifty years after first hearing them.

From 2007 to 2012, on the second Saturdays in August, I entered that same 3K race. In 2011 and 2012, I won age-group gold medals. In 2012, my time was 14:14.

"Very good for a sixty-five-year-old man," the race director said. This was a real triumph for me.

As I thought back on that triumph, a realization came to me. Having asthma was wearing the T-shirt with "limited" written on it. Now, with my success as a runner, I was beginning to feel unlimited. I began to feel I could run much faster and much farther in any kind of weather. More races, faster times, longer distances. I was excited. My running prospects seemed unlimited.

XI

A Series of Missteps

Sometimes winning results in careless overconfidence. That's what happened to me after my age-group victory in a 2012 3K race. Feeling a little bit like Superman and forgetting my asthmatic condition, I made a series of missteps.

My first misstep was taking off two weeks from running and alternative exercise after the race. The result was more congestion. After resuming running, the congestion didn't go away. Maybe a runner without asthma can get away with running twenty miles one week and zero miles the next. My asthmatic body is not like that. In the fall of 2012, I was stuck with a nagging case of chest congestion, the same old mucus in the chest.

My second misstep was increasing my running mileage too much. An increase in weekly running mileage should never be more than 5 percent a week. One week in November, I went way over 5 percent, getting lost running at a nearby state forest. While running on a trail, the trail just ended! The red arrow meant the end of the trail, not go left. I went left and got totally lost deep in the woods. I was running over logs and dead branches with absolutely no idea where I was. That was scary! Blue paint marks on trees led me to a deserted baseball field and the town dump. Desperate, I flagged down an old lady in her car.

"Please drive me back to the state-forest parking lot. I'm totally lost!"

"OK," she said, "but just to Route 112."

"Thank you so much."

By the time I finally reached my car, what started out as a four-mile run had become an eight-mile run. Way too much running for me in one day. Big mistake.

Later, I said to a friend, "Got lost running in a state forest. Reminded me of running in my teens, back in the sixties."

"How's that?" he asked.

"I was too far out, man."

My third misstep was not getting enough sleep. Eight hours a night is what my body needs. In late October, I made a weekend trip to Chicago. On Sunday, my flight back home from Chicago was delayed, so arrival at the airport wouldn't be until 2:00 a.m. With time to spare, my bright idea was to take an hour run around terminal two.

A little boy about four years old saw me and said, "You shouldn't be running!" He was right. I got back home at 4:00 a.m. and then got up at 6:00 a.m. to go to work. A lot of running and two hours' sleep. Not a good combination.

My fourth misstep was being lax about diet, not eating enough raw fruits and vegetables and not drinking enough water. Also, there was too much sugar and cheese in my diet.

My fifth misstep was exposing myself to cold air for long periods while watching football games or running. It can get very cold watching a high school football game in the stands in November. I did that for two weeks in a row. It was cold that November and I did most of my runs when the temperature was between twenty and thirty-nine degrees. I forgot that cold air can be an asthma trigger.

My sixth misstep was continuing to run when not feeling right. One Thursday in the second week of November, I felt fatigued. It would have been the perfect time to take a day off of running. But no, I figured the running would energize me. Not! Running isn't a solution for that. The runner's high that came after the run only masked my symptoms. What I needed was a nap, not a run.

My seventh misstep was running hard when under stress. That fall, I was under a lot of stress, especially in my work. I thought running really hard would alleviate stress. After one of my most stressful days, I ran three miles over rough terrain and then ran four fast four hundred-meter runs on the track. Running hard when under stress is risky. Running easy under stress is not. After that stressful day, it would have been better for me to jog two miles at a very slow pace.

My eighth misstep was running with a lot of chest congestion. When I had chest congestion that fall, I ran hard, thinking the hard running would decrease the chest congestion in my lungs. Unfortunately, that wasn't a good way to lessen my congestion.

Lack of consistency in my running, not enough sleep, too many miles, not eating the right foods every day, sitting outside a long time in the cold and running in the cold, running hard while stressed, running hard with congestion, and running when I didn't feel well. In November 2012, all these missteps were about to put me into a deep hole.

XII

Pneumonia? Not Pneumonia!

On Tuesday, November 27, 2012, I fell into that deep hole. I got pneumonia. Four days in the hospital. The entire month of December off from work. My worst illness ever. Many days in bed convalescing and wondering, *Why did this happen to me, a runner?* All my life I wanted to feel as normal as possible, to take off the T-shirt with "limited" on the front. Becoming an effective runner in my sixties helped me forget about my asthma and gave me a sense of well-being. The pneumonia took away that sense of well-being. It forced me to reexamine the relationship between my running, my health, and my entire life. It was time to start all over as a runner.

Just what is my asthma? It's a chronic condition that for me probably won't ever go away. One characteristic of asthma is that asthmatics carry more mucus in their lungs than other people. This concentration of more mucus in the lungs makes asthmatics more vulnerable to pneumonia. The pneumonia germs readily fester and grow within that mucus.

Pneumonia germs are present on a regular basis. A strong immune system fights off these germs to keep an asthmatic person (or a non-asthmatic person) pneumonia free. Anyone can get pneumonia, but with a strong immune system, my chances of getting pneumonia decrease greatly. It's a simple fact that I, as an asthmatic, have more congestion in my lungs than someone without asthma or other respiratory illnesses. With more congestion in my lungs, I was more vulnerable to pneumonia (Richard Warner, MD, in discussion with the author, January 9, 2013).

I began to realize how important it was to get rid of the congestion in my chest. After my bout with pneumonia, an inhalation-therapist friend, Yahuda Ben Moshe, told me to be sure to get rid of my mucus even if I have to swallow it! Sounds gross, but it's true (Yahuda Ben Moshe in discussion with the author, December 25, 2012).

To prevent congestion, consistency needed to be my running watchword. *My body likes consistency.* A runner with asthma, Taraschiro, helped me see the light on this very important point. On her website she talks about how important consistency is when running with asthma. It would be a good idea to go to Taraschiro's website and check this out;(http://taraschiro.wordpress.com/2011/08/13/if-youre-running-with-asthma-you-must-run-consistently). Running and doing alternative exercise on an irregular basis would only lead to more illness, as it had during my time as a school librarian in both the DC area and in the mountains. To prevent congestion from building up, it was necessary to get some exercise daily. This would help keep my immune system strong. However, it's no easy trick to exercise every day. Life has a lot of competing demands and time is short. I weighed the amount of time lost with a consistent daily exercise program against the amount of time lost with pneumonia. Actually, daily exercise saves a lot of time.

Also, appropriate nutrition helped keep my immune system strong and less vulnerable to pneumonia. I started eating more raw vegetables like spinach, broccoli, red peppers, and carrots every day. Carrots are especially important since they contain beta-carotene, a substance that helps reduce asthma symptoms. It also helped to eat a lot more foods high in antioxidants such as apples, blueberries, and strawberries. I also took 1,000 mg of vitamin C daily and made a point to eat oranges. Oranges are high in Vitamin C. Vitamin

C is a powerful antioxidant. Foods that have a lot of antioxidants may diminish asthma symptoms. Antioxidants are foods that lessen the bad effects of free radicals on the body's cells. Free radicals are created when the body metabolizes food. These free radicals attach themselves to cells in the body and damage them.

It became a habit to eat a banana after each run and drink water before and after. Bananas contain potassium, an electrolyte needed after a run to combat dehydration. It's important to prevent dehydration because dehydration can cause chest congestion. Another goal was to cut down on sugar because sugar saps energy. (Giving up my favorite snack, oatmeal cookies, was a problem. Hey, no one's perfect.) It turns out that honey is good for asthma and a good substitute for processed white sugar. Fish became my protein of choice because fish contains omega-3 fatty acids. These omega-3 fatty acids can lessen asthma symptoms. I took, along with fish, a daily fish oil pill that contained 360 mg of omega-3. Beef and chicken remained in my diet as well, but I avoided meats with a lot of fat because such foods can cause congestion.

After my bout with pneumonia, eight hours' sleep every night was a must. Getting enough sleep means real sleep, not just lying in bed, counting sheep. Doctor Warner suggested Benadryl to help me sleep better. Benadryl helped me sleep when sleeplessness was a problem.

My body needs rest from exercise as well as sleep. In fact, as a runner with asthma my body needs more rest than a non-asthmatic runner. It was Taraschiro again, who helped me realize this. On her website she points out how vital rest time is for an asthmatic runner. (http://taraschiro.wordpress.com/2011/08/13/if-youre-running-with-asthma-you-must-run-consistently). That's why I decided that each week there would be at least one day where my exercise was not strenuous. On these days, the only exercise I did was the Peaceful Warrior Workout, and that was for just four minutes. Thinking back, not taking sufficient rest days from running led to pneumonia in my late teens and again in my sixties. World-class runner Kara Goucher talks about not getting enough sleep one night and then running seventeen miles the next morning. That's fine for her, but as a runner with asthma I can't get away with that type of thing. It would make me sick.

I decided to give up being outdoors for extended periods in cold weather. No more high school football games on cold nights. Sitting in the stands on a cold night generates very little heat. Because cold air is an asthma trigger, the only cold-weather football games for me to watch became the ones on television. Running in extreme cold was something else I had to give up. Running at forty degrees and above, I could still handle. But I realized running in weather under forty degrees had become an asthma trigger for me, leading to more congestion, making me more vulnerable to pneumonia. This meant I had to rely on the treadmill for running on most winter days.

Some runners with asthma can run outdoors in cold weather. Such a runner may sometimes cover his nose and mouth when running in cold weather. He'll use neck gaiters or fleece balaclavas. Galen Rupp, an Olympic runner with asthma, wore a mask to ward off cold air when he ran the New York Half Marathon in 2011. It paid off. He finished third. Wearing something around the face can warm the air the runner inhales.

There's plenty of evidence of a link between stress and illness and between stress and asthma. Stress makes me more vulnerable to pneumonia. I'm not talking about the kind of stress where I have no control over the situation. If a hurricane is going to strike tomorrow, easy running today would probably reduce my apprehension and stress level. Or easy running after the hurricane struck would reduce my stress if the hurricane caused a lot of property damage.

But a lot of stressful things happen in my life that are not hurricanes. What about the stressful situations that I do have some control over? Stress can be lessened by communicating forthrightly and honestly with the source of the stress. It's been a process for me to learn how to do this. When working as a high school librarian, some students didn't follow rules and disrupted the library. Over time, I learned how to deal with the stress I felt when students went off task. As an example, one day a student named Johnnie wasn't doing any schoolwork and was distracting other students with loud talking. After years of trial and error regarding how to deal with this, I discovered a solution.

Instead of getting frustrated and yelling at Johnnie, ignoring him, switching his seat, or giving him detention, I walked over to him and said, "Johnnie, what assignments do you have to work on today?"

"Why do you want to know?"

"Because I'm the librarian and you're in the library."

"Whatever. Got to do a report on Abraham Lincoln. Totally gnarly," Johnnie said.

"OK, how can I help you get started?"

"Like, uh, what's the best Lincoln website?" Johnnie asked.

Johnnie was now on task. Problem solved. My stress was diminished. When dealing with stressful situations, forthright and honest communication with the source of the stress works. There's a good chance I can resolve many situations in a way that relieves my stress. Even if the problem can't be solved after discussing it with someone, the fact that I made an honest attempt to deal with the source of stress may lessen my stress. *Forthright, honest communication helps me deal with stress.* Being sneaky and less than candid leads to more stress. When I can talk about the problem with the people involved, my stress is lessened. Less stress means less vulnerability to pneumonia.

It's generally true that running helps relieve my stress. However, when my running becomes self-medication, there is the danger that my runner's high masks what's going on. It blinds me from the fact that something needs to be communicated to someone, in a forthright, honest way. If there's a problem with anyone, I need to address the problem with that person first. Then run.

My rule now is "When feeling very stressed, don't run. Take steps to diminish stress by communicating honestly with the source of the stress. Then run less and run easy." Running hard when under stress is risky. Running easy under stress is less so. After a stressful day, when I've attempted to deal with my stress, it's better for me to jog one or two miles at a very slow pace. By running a hard, grueling workout, I may have actually decreased the number of white blood cells in my system. These white blood cells are the basis for my immune system. A hard, grueling run may have also activated hormones in my system that bring on more stress. This surprising information came to me from the National Institutes of Health ("Exercise and Immunity," *MedlinePlus*, US National Library of Medicine, National Institutes of Health. Last modified May 15, 2012. http://www.nlm.nih.gov/medlineplus/ency/article/007165.htm). I'm not saying I should never do hard, grueling runs. Instead, I'm saying that when I'm under a lot of stress already, the hard run may increase my stress and seriously weaken my immune system.

In my sophomore year of college, at the beginning of cross-country season, I was going through fraternity rush. That was very stressful. Who would want me? I had a new girlfriend. Did she really like me, or what? That was stressful. I was going through an identity crisis about what type of religion I should follow. Various relatives had varying opinions on that. That was stressful. I had not done very well in my freshman year, and I was beginning my sophomore courses. That was stressful. I was also doing the hardest running of my life, logging fifty-mile weeks. I ended up with a bad case of pneumonia. That was a lesson I'd never forget. For me, with my asthma, stress has to be managed. The source of the stress has to be communicated with. As the stress increases, hard running needs to be decreased. As the stress decreases, hard running can increase. So a stressful day is a good day for me to first deal with the stress with forthright, honest communication, and then take an easy run, not a hard one.

Chest congestion is a problem very different from stress. At times I've been under little stress, not sick, and yet my chest was very congested. When faced with a lot of chest congestion, I now know, a hard, grueling run will not fix this problem. Hard runs have relieved my chest congestion temporarily. Then later that day, chest congestion increased for me. Sometimes my asthma symptoms were not severe enough to stop exercising altogether. I wasn't sick, tired, or run down. I've learned to differentiate between feeling sick and feeling some congestion in the chest. If I'm feeling sick, tired, or run down, there's no running at all. When I'm not sick, tired, or run down but have some chest congestion, I've developed a good strategy: swimming and the Peaceful Warrior Workout or *slow* running and the Peaceful Warrior Workout. It's very possible for me to feel fine and still have chest congestion. On a day like that, it's OK for me to run. It's just that it's important to not run fast. A slow run while breathing through the nose has a positive effect. After a run like that, I've had less chest congestion the next day. For me, these slow runs should never be longer than four or five miles because that's the amount of mileage I can handle without getting sick or injured. So the solution to congestion, when I'm not sick, is to maintain my training program but only do slow running, not fast.

It also helps to drink lots of water. Dehydration can cause chest congestion. Normally eight cups of water a day are needed to combat dehydration. When chest congestion happens, even more water may be needed. Fluids like water, juice and hot tea may help dilute the mucus in the chest (Adams, Abigail. "Does Drinking Water Help Chest Congestion?" *LIVESTRONG.COM*. Last updated: Jan. 28, 2015. http://www.livestrong.com/article/480208-does-drinking-water-help-chest-congestion/).

So drinking more water and slow running are strategies to ease chest congestion. On days when I'm extremely congested but not sick, I take a rest day from running, just to be on the safe side. If my congestion does not diminish in a day or two, it's time to contact my physician, Dr. Warner. Extreme congestion needs to be dealt with right away.

Part of my frustration as a young runner was that other guys could be sick with a cold and then run fast the next day. I'd get discouraged because I couldn't do that. I didn't realize then that with my asthma and congestion, it would take longer to recover from a cold. When serious chest congestion arises, it may take a few weeks for me to get back to my regular fast-running groove. That's just the way my asthma is. The point is that I will eventually get back to good running form and conditioning. Knowing that now, it does not seem like such a big problem.

I've developed a system to prevent another round of pneumonia: the Immune System Daily Score Sheet. The idea is to fill out this score sheet each day in my Runner's Diary where I record running mileage and workouts. To maintain my immune system, I need six immune-system points per day, the points as follows:

- take necessary asthma medications
- have a good night's sleep the night before and one day in the last seven days where I do only a very light workout
- get sufficient nutrition (fruits, vegetables, protein, and carbs) during the day
- not be under a great deal of stress, or if stressed, attempt to communicate with the source of stress
- not have increased running mileage by more than 5 percent a week
- not feel sick or tired that day

If all the above criteria are met, I give myself six immune system points for that day. If that's one of my running days, I go ahead and run.

Running can take a lot out of me. I may feel great after a run and have an enjoyable "runner's high," but my system may have been depleted and I need to be aware of that.

If I don't score six immune system points for a given day, there's no running that day.

Let's say I miss a lot of sleep on a Tuesday night but get the other five points. My immune system point total is only five. My immune system has been weakened, so Wednesday's hard run is canceled. I'd do some light exercising instead. This could include a mile or two of easy jogging or swimming. It would also include the Peaceful Warrior Workout that I do every day. Let's say on Friday I woke up from a good night's sleep but forgot to take my asthma meds the day before. That's only five points. No hard run on that day, light exercise instead. Let's say my daily running mileage had been three miles a day for the past month. Then my next run was twenty miles. That's way over the 5 percent increase limit. No hard run for me today. A hard run today would put my immune system at risk. Let's say each workout for seven straight days (running and nonrunning) was very strenuous. That's overdoing it. My body needs at least one light and easy workout per week to recover my strength. If I've run or exercised strenuously for six straight days, I don't run on the seventh day. Instead I do the Peaceful Warrior Workout for four minutes.

This system helps me manage my energy. It may seem ridiculous to count up these points. Someone may say, "Just use common sense."

But that's the core of the problem for the runner with asthma. What is common sense for the average person may not be common sense for me, an asthmatic. It's necessary for me to be very careful about how my energy is spent. For runners who have no chronic health problems like asthma, it's probably not as important. The Immune System Daily Score Sheet, if followed daily, enables me to get the maximum benefit from exercise with less risk of an asthma attack or pneumonia or other infection.

My personal physician, Dr. Warner, says sometimes people just get sick and there will be no clear reason why (Richard Warner MD, in discussion with the author, January 9, 2013). He is right, but using the Immune System Daily Score Sheet lessens the odds of me getting sick. After missing out on two months of running due to pneumonia in the winter of 2012–13, my plan is to score six immune system points every day.

On the next page is a blank Runner's Diary with a blank Immune System Daily Score Sheet. On the page after that is a filled-out Runner's Diary and Immune System Daily Score Sheet. My Runner's Diary is kind of like a science experiment with notes about foods eaten and other factors in my life, such as my stress level and the weather. When I notice a correlation between a food or an event and my congestion level, I note it and make necessary adjustments.

Runner's Diary Date_____

Immune System Daily Score Sheet
(One point for each, 1–6)

1. Took necessary asthma medications yesterday ___

2. A good night's sleep last night ___

3. Sufficient nutrition (fruits, vegetables, protein, carbs) yesterday ___

4. Today I am not under a great deal of stress, or if I am, I've addressed the source of stress with straightforward honest communication ___

5. Running mileage has not increased by more than 5 percent a week ___

6. I don't feel sick or tired today ___

Total___
If my score is less than six, I do not run today.

Miles run today_____
Miles run so far this week_____
PowerLung (See chapter 13 for more info on this.)_____
Peaceful Warrior Workout_____
Peak Flow before exercise
(See chapter 13 for more info on this.) _____
    after exercise_____
Notes on today's run/exercise:

John Terry McConnell

Runner's Diary Date 10-19-14

Immune System Daily Score Sheet
(One point for each, 1.-6.)

1. Took necessary asthma medications yesterday. 1

2. A good night's sleep last night 0

3. Sufficient nutrition (fruits, vegetables, protein, carbs) yesterday 1

4. Today I am not under a great deal of stress, or if I am, I've addressed the source of stress with straightforward honest communication. 1

5. Running mileage has not increased by more than 5 percent a week. 1

6. I don't feel sick or tired today. 1

Total 5

If my score is less than six, I do not run today.

Miles run today 0

Miles run so far this week 9

Slept only 5 hours last night No running today

PowerLung V Peaceful Warrior Workout

Peak Flow before exercise 340 after exercise 350

Notes on today's run/exercise:
Did Peaceful Warrior Workout

44

After a month of pneumonia, I recovered in January 2013. I consulted with my asthma doctor, Robert Ajello MD, who confirmed that my breathing was fine and I could resume my running. We discussed the possibility of reducing my asthma medications. After some tests, he determined that I needed to take Advair Diskus once a day, not twice. Ajello said one month was a quick recovery from my kind of pneumonia. He said my quick recovery was because I was a runner. It didn't seem like a quick recovery to me. It seemed like a hundred years in hell! With so little energy, I found it impossible to do just about anything. I couldn't even read. All I could do was eat, sleep, and watch TV. But this pneumonia experience was a time of much learning about running with asthma. My hope was to apply that learning in preparation for my next race.

XIII

Preparing for a 5K Race

Filling out my Runner's Diary each day gave me the confidence to effectively manage my asthma and run well. It was clear now that fewer miles run would yield better results. Too much running would put me at too much risk of getting sick and losing all my conditioning.

More alternative exercise on nonrunning days would keep my lungs in better shape for strenuous runs. Without alternative exercise the day after a run, there would be more chest congestion on the next run. Doing more alternative exercise would mean fewer miles run and less likelihood of leg injuries and less stress on my leg muscles and joints.

I developed a running plan to make me capable of running fast. Fast for me meant between eight and nine minutes per mile. I'd advise anyone with asthma to consult with their personal physician before attempting my running plan or any other running plan. Training began in earnest in June 2013. It would take about a year to get into good enough shape to run fast. I was also recovering from a knee injury, so my first two months entailed just a warm-up: easy jogging and walking. Attempts to run fast began in August 2013.

I wanted my running plan to help me reach three goals:

1. Have no illness for an entire year while preparing for this race.

2. Get a personal record of 25:59 in a 5K (3.1 mile) race. The closest I'd come in a 5K race was 26:18. Breaking the twenty-six-minute barrier would be one way to validate my new training plan.
3. Run relatively asthma free during each run for an entire year. This included the day of the race.

Here's how my plan worked.

Every day, my diet was healthy, with loads of fruits, nuts, and vegetables. I had tried various nutritional supplements, but they contained a lot of sugar. After some very painful trips to the dentist, I discontinued these supplements.

Before each run, I took two puffs of my ProAir (albuterol sulfate) inhaler fifteen minutes before the workout began. On nonrunning days, I took no ProAir. My schedule called for three runs a week and never two days in a row. Each run took between a half-hour and an hour.

Strenuous alternative exercise was done on three of my nonrunning days. After six days of running or strenuous alternative exercise, there was a rest day. On the rest day, all I did was four minutes' worth of the Peaceful Warrior Workout. The rest day was essential. Without it, my energy level would be low for the next week of running. The nonrunning strenuous alternative workouts prepared my body for the strenuous runs. These alternative workouts prepared my lungs for the next run without tiring my running muscles.

I did the Peaceful Warrior Workout every day. On nonrunning days (not counting the rest day), I also included the following exercises.

To develop abdominal muscles, I did the plank. In this exercise, the position is similar to a push-up, except that the elbows, not the hands, touch the floor. The body is kept rigid with the head aligned with the shoulders, back, and hips. This exercise is easier on the back than the traditional sit-up (Sarah Scarchilli-Janus, exercise trainer, in discussion with the author, January 8, 2014). I started by holding this position for ten seconds and worked up to holding it for one minute. It's an important exercise because the abdominal muscles play an important role in the breathing process.

The plank

While doing push-ups, the idea was to inhale while pushing up and exhale while letting the body go down. It was important to keep the body as straight as possible and keep the arms as close to the chest as possible. This helped train me to swing my arms back and forth, not side to side, while running.

The push-up

An exercise that was particularly helpful is called the bridge. To do this exercise, I laid flat on my back with my feet on the floor and my knees bent. I lifted my torso and buttocks, with my hands raised above my head and my feet on the floor. I held that position for ten seconds while holding my breath. Four reps of this was enough.

The bridge

Another exercise that helped my breathing was the snow angel. This exercise helped loosen my upper back muscles and improved my posture. As posture improves, breathing improves because the airways are straighter with good posture. I lay on my back with the small of my back pressing against the floor. My arms were at my sides and my knees were up. I moved my arms until they were over my head and then brought my arms back to my sides. My arms were on the floor at all times while doing this. I inhaled as my arms went over my head and exhaled as my arms went back to my sides. The motion is continuous, like the snow angel kids do in the snow.

Snow angel step 1   Snow angel step 2   Snow angel step 3

Snow angel step 4   Snow angel step 5

One of my favorite calisthenics was the upside down bicycle. It was one of my favorites not because I liked doing it. I did not. It was a favorite because it did me a lot of good. I stuck my legs up in the air. With my back vertical and straight, my shoulders on the ground, and my hands propping up my back, it was like riding a bicycle upside down. Gravity worked for me in this upside down exercise. The mucus at the bottom of my chest flowed down toward my throat. When doing this exercise, I coughed up a lot of mucus. I kept a handkerchief handy. This exercise cleared my chest. The upside down bicycle forced me to breath hard, the way a running sprint would. But unlike a running sprint, this exercise is very easy on leg muscles and joints. (I've occasionally used stationary bicycles and elliptical trainers for alternative exercise. I like the upside down bicycle better because it gives me a better cardiovascular workout.)

The upside down bicycle

After doing the upside down bicycle for a minute or two, I'd do ten V-ups. The V-up is an exercise from the Peaceful Warrior Workout. To do a V-up, you lay flat on your back, inhale, lift up your torso and legs at the same time with your arms forward, exhale, and bring your torso and legs back to the floor. In the middle of doing a V-up, the body forms the letter V. It's kind of a wide V, but a V nonetheless. It's good if you can keep your legs straight, but it's not necessary if that's hard to do. The V-up is one of the best deep breathing exercises I know of and deep breathing is vital for running with asthma.

First step, V-up

Second step, V-up

Third step, V-up

After the V-ups I'd do some push-ups, usually ten.

These exercises really helped my cardiovascular fitness. I'd do them in sets: upside down bicycle, V-ups, and push-ups. In a typical workout, I'd do between five and fifteen sets of these exercises. (After doing this regimen of exercises for a year my right shoulder got really sore. So I stopped doing sets of ten push-ups as part of the regimen. Instead, I did just one set of twenty push-ups. The soreness in my right shoulder went away.)

I did all these exercises on nonrunning days. These exercises prepared my lungs for a strenuous run the next day. I'd often cough up a lot of mucus doing these exercises. Then, when I'd run the next day, I'd have very little chest congestion. *I was clearing out my lungs, making the next day's strenuous run possible.*

The beauty of these exercises is that they don't make me sweat much. This is very different from a strenuous run, where I sweat like crazy. These workouts prepare me for the next day's run without draining my strength, the way a strenuous run would.

On running days, each run began with a mile of slow warm-up jogging. Running hard at the beginning of a run is risky. I learned this lesson the hard way. In February 2013, not doing easy jogging before running fast contributed to a knee injury that prevented me from running for four months.

The last part of the warm-up called for some hard sprints, two strenuous two hundred-meter runs, and then sometimes one strenuous four hundred-meter run. These bursts of hard running worked extremely well to prevent asthma symptoms from coming up later during the most strenuous part of the running workout.

After the warm-up jog and the sprints, the most strenuous part of the running workout was next. The following are some examples.

On some days, no more than once a week, it was interval training of five to six four hundred-meter runs around a track or four eight hundred-meter runs around a track with between ninety seconds and two minutes of rest between each run. This is something I could have never done when my running program started again in 2006. It would have made me sick then. It was necessary to slowly build up to running fast. In 2006, I ran slowly for two months before even trying to run fast. By the spring of 2007, interval training became part of my weekly routine.

Another type of strenuous running is called *fartlek*. *Fartlek* means speed play in Swedish. In this type of run, I'd cover two to four miles varying the pace constantly. It was speed up or slow down, depending on how fast I wanted to run. At times, that would be as fast as possible. At other times, it would be a little-slower pace, and at other times a jog. After running a rigorous interval workout, it was fun to make the next run a *fartlek*.

Another option was hill work. Very convenient, since I live on a hill. It was like this: run up the hill for one hundred- to four hundred-meters and then jog back down. Usually, after five or ten trips up the hill, the workout was done. These runs improved my breathing more than any other runs.

Another type of run was a time trial. After the warm-up, I'd run from one to three miles for time. Sometimes I did it on a four hundred-meter track. At other times, I did it on a country road, away from traffic. The odometer on my car helped me figure out the start and end points of these runs. Time trials gave me a sense of how my running program was progressing. With my Timex Ironman Triathlon watch, I timed these runs. That my time improved gave me confidence that my running was getting faster. The time trials also helped me figure out if my race preparation strategy was working. Was I getting the right balance and sequence between rest days and strenuous workouts? When my time on my Timex Ironman Triathlon watch showed improvement, the answer was "yes."

On some days, I did long, slow distance training. My pace might speed up a little after the warm-up, but not much. These runs would gradually increase over a year's time from three miles to five. Long, slow distance training improves a runner's strength and endurance.

After a strenuous run, it's a good idea to do a five-minute warm-down jog when the hard work is over.

To prepare for a race, my hardest workouts were done three and four weeks before the race. With two weeks to go, I ran a little easier. For example, instead of running six four hundred-meter interval runs it was four. Instead of running four eight hundred-meter interval runs, it was three. The week of a race, there'd be a strenuous run three days before the race, a nonstrenuous rest day with only an easy Peaceful Warrior Workout two days before the race, and a strenuous alternative exercise workout (swimming, if possible) one day before the race. On the alternative-exercise workout the day before the race, swimming twelve laps of the pool and treading water for ten minutes worked best. Taking a rest day the day before the race may work for people without asthma, but not for me in 2014. My rest day was two days before the race. All I did on that day was the Peaceful Warrior Workout for five minutes. This race preparation may seem odd. It seems odd to me. Yet, when I did it, my lungs and my entire body worked great on race day.

When my training began after coming back from a knee injury in June 2013, six miles was my weekly total. Gradually my running increased to twelve miles a week. Earlier, between 2007 and 2012, I was covering up to seventeen miles a week. This sometimes led to illness. My plan was to run no more than twelve miles a week in order to avoid illness.

In January 2014, it became a daily practice to blow into a peak flow meter to determine how effectively my lungs were working. The score on the meter showed the power of my breath. A score of 325 meant my breathing was OK. A score of 350 meant my breathing was very good. A score under 310 showed my breathing was not good, and there would be no running that day. (A given score that was good for me might not be good for someone else. Each person is different.) The peak flow meter helped me know when not to run

(Karin Purugganan, inhalation therapist, in discussion with the author, January 2013).

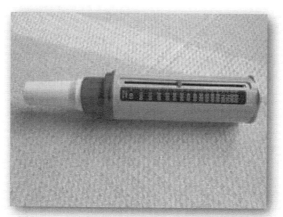

The Mini-Wright Peak Flow Meter

I ordered my peak flow meter from MiniWrightPeakFlowMeter. com for under thirty-five dollars. It's the same type of peak flow meter my asthma doctor uses. My peak flow scores from the doctor's office could be meaningfully compared to scores from home. Scores can vary from one brand of peak flow meter to another.

My asthma doctor, Robert Ajello, MD suggested I try another device, called PowerLung, to improve my breathing. This is a handheld device. The idea is to inhale forcefully for three seconds, pause for two seconds, and exhale forcefully for three seconds. The degree of difficulty for the breath can be adjusted by using the inhale and exhale dials. The makers of PowerLung suggest doing three sets of ten breaths twice a day. The PowerLung information guide claims that if this device is used as directed, diaphragm muscles will become stronger in three to four weeks. In my case, this proved to be true. Doing PowerLung made my breathing easier and made it easier for me to run at a strenuous pace. After I did PowerLung for a week in February 2014, my time in a two-mile run was the fastest in a year and a half. I checked my scores on the Mini-Wright Peak Flow Meter for the first five weeks of PowerLung use. I then compared the average score of the first week with the average score of the fifth week. Thanks to PowerLung, my peak flow score increased 14.6 percent from the first week to the fifth week. PowerLung did not get rid of my chest congestion. Instead, it strengthened the muscles in my diaphragm and made breathing easier, with or without congestion. The PowerLung costs $149 and is available at PowerLung.com.

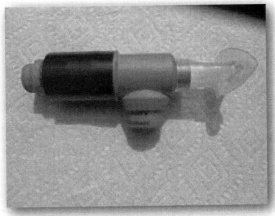
Powerlung

I sometimes swam and treaded water as an alternative exercise to running. Water exercise has made it easier for me to breathe while running. Swimming the day before a race made me congestion free for the next day's race. On the Mini-Wright Peak Flow Meter, after swimming for twenty minutes, treading water for ten minutes, and sitting in a hot tub for three minutes, my lung function improved by 14 percent from a reading taken the same day prior to exercise. Swimming, especially in warm water, increased the humidity inside my lungs, making asthma symptoms less likely. Swimming reju-venated my body, improved my breathing, and gave me a sense of well-being. It was the perfect exercise to do to prepare for the next day's run. If swimming isn't an option, a hot shower can reduce asthma symptoms. Whenever possible, I try to swim on alternate exercise days. In 2014, for a runner with asthma like me, swimming was the best alternative exercise possible the day before a race. When swimming is not possible, doing sets of upside down bicycle, and V-ups is the next best thing.

Since May 2013, I've been doing tai chi daily for at least five minutes a day. This, too, has helped reduce my asthma symptoms while running. Tai chi improves breathing capacity, encourages proper breathing through the nose, and relaxes the muscles, including the muscles around the airways. The training DVDs of Dr. Paul Lam (1-800-283-7800) were helpful in learning tai chi.

Another method for relaxing my muscles was the Feldenkrais Method. When I did Feldenkrais Method exercises, my muscles, including breathing muscles, were significantly relaxed. As a result, I ran stronger and breathed easier after a session of Feldenkrais. As with tai chi, these exercises involve slow movement of muscles. More information on the Feldenkrais Method can be obtained at FeldenkraisInstitute.com.

On the next page is a diagram of the lung. I visualized that diagram every day, imagining that my breathing tubes were straight, my breathing muscles relaxed, my airway walls expanded, the air running through my airways warm and moist, and the mucus in my airways minimal.

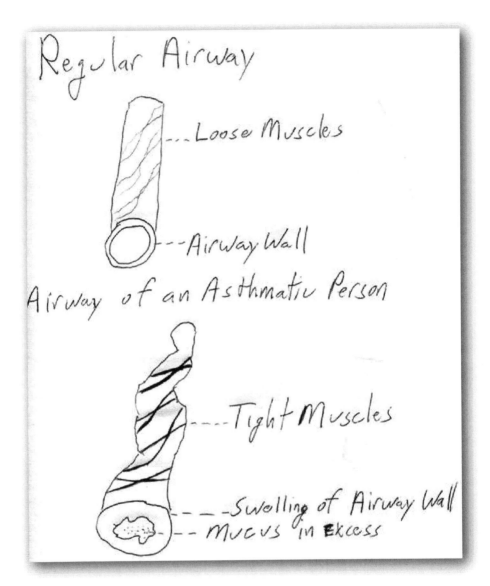

I also visualized healing in my lungs, not getting sick, running a strong race, and setting a new personal record for a 5K on June 7, 2014. Visualization was a matter of focusing my mind to imagine good outcomes. I spent a few minutes visualizing these good outcomes every day.

In May 2014, I registered online for a 5K race that was scheduled for June 7. For me, it was the perfect race to run. It took place a year after my training began. It was close to home and easy to get to. The entry fee went to benefit a favorite charity, prevention of substance abuse.

Three weeks before the race, I developed some lung irritation. A friend asked, "Do you have a cold?"

"No, just a little asthma."

My peak flow scores remained the same. My strenuous workouts continued. But my lungs didn't feel quite as good as they should. After thinking about this for a few days, it became clear that the problem was the air pollution in Chicago, where I'd been running outdoors. Chicago had become my temporary home due to a family illness. Fortunately, I'd soon be going back to the cleaner air in my rural mountain home. The best solution was to do my last run in Chicago indoors on a treadmill. The lung irritation went away a few days after my return home.

I did the following things to keep my immune system strong so I could train for a year leading up to my 5K race: less running per week than before my recent pneumonia, alternative exercise, PowerLung, Feldenkrais, tai chi, visualization, the Runner's Diary, and indoor running as needed. For my plan to work, it had to be followed consistently, every day. My goal was to break twenty-six minutes in a 5K race. In my thirties, my 5K times had been way under twenty-six minutes, but my age was now sixty-seven. The question was "Could I do it?"

XIV

Race Day

On Saturday, June 7, 2014 I needed no alarm clock to wake up for the 5K race. With great anticipation, I scrambled out of the house about 8:00 a.m. and drove ten miles to the race site. The day before the race, I swam twelve laps in the local YMCA pool. Two days before the race, I'd taken a rest day with a very nonstrenuous Peaceful Warrior Workout. After a year of consistent training, it was time to let it all hang out and see what the outcome would be.

I showed up at the race about an hour and a half before the 10:00 a.m. start with no breakfast in my stomach. Eating before running doesn't work for me. It takes about six hours for the food to be sufficiently digested. I thought back to a 2.55-mile race I'd run four years ago. I ate a turkey sandwich three hours before the race. That sandwich made its presence known to me during all 2.55 miles. That was one slow and disappointing race. After that race, I made a rule: no protein before a race or a training run. When the running is finished, I get all the protein I want. After today's race, my reward would be a steak, if my watch registered under twenty-six minutes.

My prerace preparation on race day was as follows: (1) five minutes—taking two puffs of ProAir (albuterol sulfate) inhaler, drinking sixteen ounces of water, and figuring out where to leave my car keys and sports bag; (2) five minutes—the Peaceful Warrior Workout and some other breathing exercises; (3) thirty minutes of running, slow running, and then a strenuous four-hundred-meter sprint; (4) five minutes—bathroom break; 5) five minutes—stretching; and (6) ten minutes—reporting to starting line, relaxing, walking around, drinking more water, retying shoes, and talking to other runners. The last twenty minutes before the race were for relaxation. This whole process of a warm-up run and then twenty minutes of rest and relaxation before the race is called the refractory effect. One version of this approach is a thirty-minute, slow-running warm-up and then twenty minutes of rest before the race. Another successful approach is to do seven thirty-second sprints with a two-and-one-half-minute rest between each sprint followed by twenty minutes of rest. Both of these approaches have improved the running performance of asthmatics (Jonathan Brostoff and Linda Gamlin, *Asthma: The Complete Guide to Integrative Therapies*, Rochester, VT: Healing Arts Press, 2000). My approach was to combine elements of both methods in my warm-up—the slow run and the sprint. Hopefully my version of the refractory effect would improve my performance in the race today.

As I waited for the starting gun to go off, my mind drifted back to Gordie Howe, the ice hockey player for the Detroit Red Wings, the greatest athlete I ever met. His words to us at the sports banquet fifty years ago reverberated in my head. "If someone beats you at tennis, don't shake his hand. Look at him in the eye and say, 'Next time, I'll beat you.'"

What did Howe's words mean for me now? Waiting for the starting gun, a moment of clarity seemed near.

Bang! The race began. The moment of clarity was on hold. It was time to concentrate on breathing and making my legs move fast. I hit "start" on the Ironman Triathlon watch on my right arm. To reach my goal of 25:59, it would take an 8:20 pace for each mile. That would mean going out fast.

I started out fast, ahead of a guy named Duffy, a very capable runner. There was no mile marker and that disoriented me. The second mile went slower, but the pace was still fairly fast. Other people were passing me, including Duffy, but so what? My pace was still strong. In the third mile, I "hit the wall." My energy was gone. Right before an armory that looked like a medieval castle, the race went up a hill. It felt like the longest hill in the history of mankind. (Driving by that hill months after the race, it didn't seem like much of a hill at all.) All I could do was keep going, staying twenty yards behind Bob, the guy in front of me. He was a big balding guy about ten years younger than me, with gray hair and a big stomach. It looked like he was running slowly, which meant my speed was even slower. I really wanted to run faster to catch up to him, but there was no way. The energy just wasn't there. It took all my willpower just to keep going. Before the race, I anticipated having many negative thoughts during the last mile, when the going got toughest. When the last mile came, my only thought was, "God, is 5K a long way or what?" When we hit the home stretch with two hundred yards to go, it was time to surge past Bob to the finish. The energy to do that just wasn't there. As I hit the finish line, with Bob still in front of me, the race official called out, "27:27."

XV

Getting More Visual for the Next Race

It didn't dawn on me until the next day that I'd had absolutely no asthma symptoms during the race. Well, that was something positive. The race also revealed what I needed to work on—gaining more endurance for the third mile of the course.

A few weeks after the race, a friend gave me a reflexology, acupressure, and Reiki treatment. Lying on the Reiki portable massage table, eyes closed, fully awake, I wondered, *What's going on here?*

After the session was over, I experienced a tremendous surge of energy and a renewed sense of well-being. My peak flow reading for that day immediately increased from 335 to 370. My deep breaths were deeper. Reiki worked for me. I'd advise anyone with asthma to consult with their personal physician before trying it.

This successful Reiki experience emboldened me to run another 5K race on Tuesday, July 1. The race would be on a wooded trail about an hour's drive from my house. It would also be a social event because a friend, Ted, would meet me at the race, and we'd have hamburgers after. The burgers would be a real treat.

Inspired by the results of reflexology, acupressure, and Reiki on the massage table, I created a new visualization for myself as follows.

Warm, moist air flows into my lungs, down my breathing tubes, expanding, relaxing, straightening, and healing them. There's less mucus in my chest. Energy surges from my lungs to my heart to all my muscles.

I wrote down this visualization on a piece of paper, put it in my wallet for reference, and memorized it. This would be my mantra to repeat to myself during the race.

Between June 7 and July 1, my diet changed. Not only was there no red meat, there was almost no white sugar. OK, a Dunkin' Donuts decaf coffee with cream and sugar a few times. How could anybody resist that? For me it's the best drink on the planet. And a few cookies. Just a few. I started drinking beet juice every morning. Beet juice by itself is kind of gross, so I added carrots, a handful of spinach, two green apples, ice, and water. All these ingredients were mixed in a Vitamix machine (Vitamix.com). The Vitamix is great for juicing because it utilizes the entire fruit or vegetable. There is no leftover pulp. Of course, I cored the apples and peeled the carrots before I put them in the Vitamix. The green apples cancel out that super sweet beet taste. When I first started drinking beet juice, it gave me indigestion. I was using a whole beet. A naturopathic doctor friend of mine, Jim Lemkin, suggested I use only one or two slices of a beet when I prepared my beet juice. This prevented the indigestion (Jim Lemkin in discussion with the author, November 14, 2014). This drink supplies me with energy for the entire day. Beets have magnesium. This is a very important mineral for people with asthma, and it turned out that magnesium was available in foods already in my diet: spinach, almonds, almond butter, cashews, and broccoli. With the beet juice, more magnesium, no red meat, very little sugar, and a lot of swimming along with the running, I was beginning to feel like an athlete again—breathing easily, feeling strong, and ready to race.

Two days after the Reiki, reflexology, acupressure, and beet juice, I ran a workout of four eight hundred-meter runs with two-and-a-half minutes' rest in between each run. Compared to the same workout done a week earlier, my total time improved by twenty-eight seconds. Four days before the race, I did two repeat miles in 8:45 and 8:53 with a two-and-a-half minute rest in between. Not that fast a pace. It wouldn't be a fast enough pace to break twenty-six minutes in my next 5K race, but it would be fast enough for a significant improvement over my 27:27 on June 7.

I left nothing to chance preparing for this race. I dusted the house a few days before the race. I wasn't going to let dust in my house stop me from running well. Even though it was now summer, my bedroom window was closed at night. At my mountain home, it can get down to fifty degrees at night in the summer. It wouldn't be good to breathe cold air while sleeping because cold air is one of my asthma triggers.

The race for July 1 was set for 6:30 p.m., not the best time of day for me to run. However, July 1 was the day that fit my schedule. Later in the month, there'd be no time for a race.

I followed a training plan with a rest day two days before the race and a swim one day before. On race day at about 3:30 p.m., I swam and treaded water for fifteen minutes. Once, a couple of years ago, swimming right before a two-mile time trial helped me run a fast time. After swimming, I showered and headed for the race site, about an hour away via country roads.

When I got to the race site at about 5:15 p.m., the weather was hot and sticky. My usual warm-up made me feel lethargic. With twenty minutes to go before the race, I joked around with a friend, perfect for refractory time before a race. Then...

Bang! The gun went off and the race was on.

Like the last race, my start was too fast. Maybe it was the heat. At the mile mark, my time was 4:15. Feeling disoriented, I wondered, "How could it be?"

It was really the half-mile mark. My energy was fading quickly. By a mile and a half, all my energy just disappeared. Jogging was all my body could handle. That mantra I had planned to repeat to myself while running? Forget about it. I was too exhausted to repeat anything to myself except "I'm so tired." The running trail was beautiful, but my running felt ugly. I struggled to the finish line in 31:55.

XVI

Change in Gratitude, Change in Attitude

What had gone wrong? First, my swim two hours before the race was an unnecessary warm-up. It robbed me of energy for the race. Second, morning is the best time for a person with asthma to run. It was a waste of my time running a race in the evening.

A week later, I did a time trial for a 5K run on a nearby track. My prerace preparation was different this time: a rest day three days before, some four hundred-meter runs two days before, and a swim one day before. This worked a lot better. My time was 27:30, but more importantly I felt great. My pace was just under nine-minute miles for the entire race and my finish was strong. I avoided the agony of having no energy for the last mile. This time trial was a real confidence booster. Because of my prerace preparation, my body was ready to run that day. This would be my prerace preparation for my next race.

A couple of weeks later in a time trial of 4/5 of a mile up a hill, I forgot to take my ProAir inhaler and ran my best time ever for that course by forty-one seconds. That was a first for me. It was beginning to look like my body was getting into good running shape.

During a weekend in early August, I had an epiphany. It started with a deep-sea fishing trip with my friend Eric. On a fishing boat off the Atlantic coast, we caught five fish. The biggest was a thirty-five-inch bluegill. Catching five fish was a first. Previous fishing trips had been totally unsuccessful. I had planned that the fishing trip would be a rest day for me. Not! It was actually quite grueling. The boat moved around a lot to find the best spot for fishing. We loaded bait and cast our fishhooks into the water at least fifty times! When the bluegill bit, it took all my strength and what seemed like a long time to pull him in.

My first realization was the process of running, fishing, or any other sport was more important than the product. It was more fun to just enjoy doing it rather than constantly striving for a personal record, whether it's the biggest fish or the fastest time.

The second part of the epiphany came a week later at a family reunion. A few days prior to that event, I'd taken too long on a run. I didn't tell the person I was with how long the run would take. This resulted in inconveniencing that person. Why did that happen? Running had become a huge part of my being. It was running that enabled me to feel like a less limited, more normal person. Running enabled me to feel as capable as anyone else. That process has been going on since age fourteen, when I began to run. That was totally OK, but my running was beginning to matter more than important people in my life. That was crazy. I needed to get my priorities straight. Running should not have been my top priority. Relations with family and friends were way ahead of running. The next day at the family reunion, I witnessed the power of love. It was a relative's birthday (she had turned ninety), and it was amazing to witness the love poured out to this relative. After dinner at a splendid and scenic bed-and-breakfast place, we were sitting in a large circle in a comfortable parlor, telling jokes and laughing. What could be better than that? When I'm ninety, wouldn't it be nice for me to experience my own birthday party that way? If my first priority is family and friends, maybe that will happen. My relationships with family and friends made me strong. Yes, running made me strong, too, but when running harmed these relationships, my attitude about running had to change, because the relationships were more important.

So I began to practice appreciating the people in my life more than running. Running wasn't my top priority; family and friends were.

Someone said, "You do a Runner's Diary every day. If relationships are so important to you, why don't you do a relationships diary?"

"Hmm," I said. "Sounds like a good topic for another book."

But that person had a point. There's the danger that my running gets me too self-centered. My personal best time on the stopwatch, my correct diet, my sufficient sleep, my need to fit my running program into the schedules of others, my personal battle against dust, animal dander, and other asthma triggers—my, my, my. It gets a little old. What about the people in my life? With all this focus on my running, how did John Terry McConnell integrate running with the people in the rest of his life? They were way more important than running. But if I screwed up my relationships with others, that would have led to more stress and illness, and no running at all. The art of compromise came in here. On Monday, I wanted to run four miles in fifty minutes. However, three miles in thirty-five minutes worked better with my schedule and the people I was close to. So on Monday, I didn't run the extra mile, and my life was less stressed. I am a runner with asthma and to do this it takes a lot of determination. But when my determination overlooks the needs of others and my own welfare, it becomes compulsion. Compulsive behavior does more harm than good.

Don Henley's song "The Boys of Summer" kept playing in the back of my mind. It was Tuesday, August 26, 2014. Summer was quickly slipping through my hands. Today, the teachers were returning to the school where I once worked. It was early, 7:00 a.m., when my friend Bill showed up at the school track to run with me. We were going to run a 5K race together, just the two of us. Bill is a much stronger runner, so he was going to pace me as I tried for a personal record. First, we did a mile warm-up and a four hundred-meter run at a fast pace. In the three days leading up to today, my preparation had been perfect: a rest day three days ago, a few four-hundreds two days ago, and swimming yesterday.

It was about 7:35 a.m. when I looked at my watch and said, "Bill, if we start the race now, you won't be late for work."

"OK," he said.

I pressed the start button on my Ironman Triathlon watch, and we were off. Bill was in the second lane on my right shoulder, keeping pace with me, step for step. We hit the four hundred-meter mark at 1:53, too fast. *No way I can keep this pace up*, I thought.

At the mile mark, my time was 8:12, right on pace for a new personal record, but my thoughts weren't optimistic. *This pace is impossible*, I thought. *Better stop. Who cares about personal records?*

At the mile-and-a-half mark, self-doubt seemed to be in control. *God, only half done and so tired. Maybe I should quit.*

At the two-mile mark, some optimism crept into my mind. *Too much invested in this to quit now, and besides, my breathing is perfect.* Two-thirds done.

Bill was still right with me, and he didn't seem the least bit tired. He was saying hi to three women walking around the track. I kept quiet, not having the energy to do anything but keep running. At least my pace was still relatively fast, not jogging. And my body didn't feel the agony of the last mile, like it had on June 7 and July 1. Again, my long and complicated mantra about warm moist air flowing through my breathing tubes… It totally slipped my mind. That mantra worked fine doing visualization in bed at night. Running today, it was too tiring to even think of it. My new mantra was just simple counting- one, two, three, four, etc.

At the finish, after 3.1 miles, my time was 26:32. Not a new personal record, but my best time since my bout with pneumonia two years ago, a fifty-five-second improvement over my June 7 5K. My continued improvement validated my plan for running with asthma. The sequence of rest day three days before the race, four hundred- meter interval runs two days before the race, a swim one day before the race, and then race day really worked well for me. The warm-up four hundred-meter run at 1:44 was amazing, considering that two days earlier, trying my hardest, my best time at that distance was eleven seconds slower. Running in the morning today was another factor. Morning really is better for runners with asthma. Two days earlier, those four hundred- meter runs had been done in the afternoon. My plan worked. No doubt, in August 2014, my lungs really needed the sequence of rest day, four hundred-meter runs day, and then swimming the day before a race. Quite different from most runners, who rely on a rest day one day before a race.

I thanked Bill, and he went off to work. He was a big help, and we'll run together again.

I had a lot of gratitude that at as a man in my sixties, my running could continue. I was even more grateful for the wonderful love and support of family and friends. Running the extra mile to make the personal record possible is not half as important as "running the extra mile" to maintain strong relationships with family and friends. Balancing running with life reminds me of Kenny Rogers' song, "The Gambler." When the cards are in my favor, that's a good time to run long and hard. When the cards don't look so good, it's best to run less or not at all.

XVII

Goals

Meatloaf has a song titled "Two Out of Three Ain't Bad." It was now close to two years after my pneumonia and for me, like Meatloaf, it was two out of three.

After my bout with pneumonia I had three goals:

1. One of my goals was to run for a year without being sick. From June 2013 to September 2014, I'd done just that. The Immune System Daily Score Sheet in the Runner's Diary has six elements (appropriate sleep, rest days, nutrition, running mileage, stress handling, and asthma medications). Maintaining these six elements had worked. The elasticity of my lungs had been improved by my strenuous exercise. The proof was improved peak flow scores. The fact that I didn't run too much helped prevent illness. My training can continue with the goal of improving as a runner. Getting sick for a few months would have made that impossible. Goal one: check.

2. The second goal was to break twenty-six minutes for the 5K distance. On August 25, 2014, I was only fourteen seconds off my personal record (as a man in my sixties) and thirty-three seconds off my goal. Real improvement! There will be other races to try to set a personal best.

3. The third goal was to run for an entire year and run 5K races with little or no asthma. From June 2013 to August 2014 I had less chest congestion than at any other time in my life. From June 2013 to August 2014 there was not one run where my asthma made my running difficult. But these 5Ks could have been a different story. One of my worst fears was that asthma symptoms would appear during a race. During both of these 5Ks, I had no breathing problems. My asthma symptoms had been negligible for over a year of running. Goal three: check.

Epilogue

Looking back on a lifetime's love of sports, I found this love to have been a blessing and a curse. A curse because it contributed to my feeling of being limited because of my asthma. A blessing because it made me determined to be a good athlete and a good runner. Running has helped me maintain good health and significantly reduced my asthma symptoms.

The Peaceful Warrior Workout has also reduced my asthma symptoms. Recently, I had chest congestion in the middle of the night. It was difficult to breathe and impossible to sleep. I did the Peaceful Warrior Workout for four minutes and then went back to bed. My congestion was considerably reduced. The deep breathing exercises in this workout have worked wonders for me!

I'd given up running a couple of times: after my sophomore year of college and after the marathon in DC in my late thirties. Never again. Now I know how important it is for me to run consistently, for my health and my spirit. I've begun to recapture the determination Coach Ambrose taught me in high school.

I started running again at age fifty-nine, and it's been a great success. I couldn't have done this without the support of my medical doctors, Richard Warner, MD and Robert Ajello, MD. Their support of my running program gave me the confidence to do it. I knew with each step that my running program was improving my health, not making it worse. I'd advise anyone with asthma to develop a strong working relationship with their personal physician before they begin a running program.

Looking back on a life of running with asthma, I think for me there are three stages. In stage one, by doing the Peaceful Warrior Workout and other breathing exercises, my breathing improved significantly. In stage two, I was able to handle slow running. As my muscles got stronger I could begin to tackle longer distances. In stage three, I could do fast runs for short distances, like a quarter-mile, and gradually build up to fast runs at longer distances, like a 3K or 5K. By following the six principles of the Immune System Daily Score Sheet in my Runner's Diary, I was able to stay healthy enough to continue running.

It was a snowy and cold Thursday in February, 2015. Way too cold to run outdoors. Lately, I'd been running on a treadmill at the nearest YMCA. I'd recently discovered that running too fast on the treadmill causes knee problems for me. To get a good running workout, I now slow my speed to 5 to 6 mph and increase the incline on the treadmill to three or four. That way I get a good workout without leg problems. On alternative-exercise days, I found a new exercise to go with the upside down bicycle, V-ups, and push-ups. It's called a burpee. A set of burpees is a strong cardiovascular challenge. To do a burpee, you do a push-up and then stand up and jump as high as you can. I'd been doing ten sets of the following: one hundred rotations on the upside down bicycle, ten V-ups, and five burpees. Then I increased to ten burpees per set. These burpees had a special effect on me. After doing sixty of them, I could feel my lungs expanding. Breathing became especially free and easy. For an asthmatic like me, that's a special, wonderful feeling. These alternative-exercise workouts are not fun the way a run is. But they sure do get me ready for the next day's run. I'd been able to run at a strong pace, asthma free.

There was a down side to doing burpees. They were great for my lungs and terrible for my knees, so I stopped doing them. Then my knee pain went away, almost immediately. This is part of running with asthma: the awareness of what my body can handle and what it can't. So I avoided an exercise that caused me knee problems. It's probably a great exercise for someone else but not for me.

Inside me, the tension between Apollo and Dionysus (between discipline and cravings) continues. Every once in a while, I'm tempted to smoke but the knowledge of how much it would hurt my running prevents me from doing it. Pizza is another matter. Yes, eating pizza creates mucus in my lungs. Recently I said to myself, "Well, one or two slices won't hurt anything." One or two slices turned into six or seven. I couldn't stop myself. I felt like the character Comte de Reynaud played by Alfred Molina in the movie *Chocolat*. Molina's character is trying to resist eating chocolate for Lent. He goes out of control when he breaks into a chocolate shop, and eats so much chocolate he passes out. The way that character loved chocolate is the way I love pizza. After eating too much pizza one recent evening, the mucus in my lungs increased for two weeks. With determination I continue to resist pizza. But probably not as effectively as it would be for Apollo!

Another thing I used to love and had to give up was milk shakes. As a fifteen-year-old I drank milk shakes every chance I got, hoping I'd gain weight for football. I never gained any weight, but did I love those milk shakes, At age sixteen I realized that milk shakes caused my chest to get congested so I stopped drinking them. Recently I discovered that combining a ripe banana, almond milk, ice, and a couple of slices of a beet in the Vitamix makes a great tasting milk shake with no milk. It's like drinking Apollo and Dionysus at the same time.

There were other, faster runners in my age group at 2014's June 7 and July 1 races. What about the importance of winning? I thought about what Gordie Howe meant in his speech to our team, fifty-one years ago.

Howe is now in his late eighties, retired, and living in Bloomfield Hills, Michigan, about five miles from where I grew up. It would be an amazing experience to talk to him and ask him just what he meant when he said, "Ten years from now if a guy beats you at tennis, don't shake his hand. Look him in the eye and say, 'Next time, I'll beat you.'" I probably will not have that opportunity. The best I can do is figure out what his speech means for me. My life has had its share of wins and losses and successes and failures in every realm—sports, relationships, business, career, and more. After each future success or failure in whatever I'm attempting to do, I'll look life in the eye and say, "Next time, I'll do it better." And mean it. Whether Howe meant that or not, that's what I got out of his speech. Remembering Howe's speech, one thing stands out: the words "don't shake his hand." Perhaps Howe was saying social graces are not anywhere near as important as the intention, deep in the heart, to do better next time. I'm looking forward to future races and my goal is still to run a 5K in under twenty-six minutes. I know, the process of running is a lot more important than any time on my Ironman Triathlon stopwatch. Yet, that goal looms like a mountain in the distance. Coach Ambrose's words still resonate inside me. "You have no idea how good a runner you could be." I couldn't be a runner with asthma without the determination that Ambrose taught me.

A guy I knew on the cross-country team in high school was a world-class runner. He had a great gift, running one of the fastest miles ever for a prep runner. What's my gift? To be a runner managing asthma well and running well. It turns out that in the 2012 Olympics in London, seven hundred athletes were diagnosed with asthma. Those athletes were two times more likely to win medals than the athletes without asthma! Asthmatic Galen Rupp's silver medal in the ten thousand-meter run comes to mind. Perhaps the surprising Olympic success of asthmatic athletes comes from the fact that athletes with asthma know they need to do a very thorough warm-up right before their event to diminish asthma symptoms. Perhaps they perform better because of their superior warm-up the day of the competition.

So as an asthmatic man in my late sixties, I've learned to do a better warm-up, leading to a real advantage for me when running. It's nice to have an advantage, yet it doesn't matter to me now if anyone else is a faster runner, is smarter, better looking, funnier, or more popular, or has a richer bank account than me. No, none of that matters. I've got my gift, and there's no need to compare it with anyone else's.

My gift is running well with asthma.

Recently, I read the book *The Perks of Being a Wallflower*, written by Stephen Chbosky and I saw the movie. The story gave me goose bumps as I witnessed the way the main characters, Sam (played by Emma Watson) and Charlie, overcame their limits. Sam and Charlie both talk about feeling "infinite" as they ride on the tunnel and the bridge in Pittsburgh, standing up on the cargo bay of Sam's pickup truck (not at the same time). The song "Just for One Day (Heroes)" is playing in the background. Sam and Charlie's "infinite" feeling reminds me of my wish to be "unlimited" in my running. Running grueling fifty-mile weeks in any kind of weather and setting age-group records in the 5K. Well, that would be infinite and unlimited for me, but it wouldn't be reality for me, running with asthma. No, I can forget about that dream. But there's another dream that's become a reality. I can now take off that T-shirt with the word "limited" written on the front. Running well and breathing well make me feel much less limited, but not unlimited. The memory of pneumonia illuminates the knowledge that my running with asthma has serious limits. Within those limits, as I train for the next race, I feel just a little "infinite" and "unlimited."

Author's Note

One of the purposes of treating asthma is to enable the asthmatic to lead a healthy lifestyle that includes physical exercise ("Exercise and Asthma." *WebMD*. Last modified 2015. http://www.webmd.com/asthma/guide/exercising-asthma).

What exercise and how much exercise is something you and your medical doctor should consider together. Please consult with your physician before beginning this or any other exercise program. If you and your doctor conclude that distance running would be good for you, I hope this book helps you run.

In this book I emphasized the importance of applying deep breathing techniques before starting a running program. I've never done yoga but I've found many sources that extol the virtues of yoga to promote better breathing.

All athletes with asthma have their ups and downs when attempting to deal with this chronic condition. This even includes the great distance runner Galen Rupp. He's had to drop out of races a few times because of illness including asthma attacks.

It was April of 2015 and I was putting the finishing touches on this book. I'd followed all the principles laid down in my Immune System Daily Score Sheet that month and yet, I got a very bad case of chest congestion. Just walking a block tired me out. My running ceased. My peak flow score was as low as 250. After reviewing old peak flow scores in my Runner's Diary I realized that I needed a 310 peak flow score to be able to run. A score under 310 indicated severe congestion. A score under 310 was a red flag for me. Such a score meant that it was time to call Dr. Warner so he could treat my severe chest congestion with appropriate medication.

I felt better for a few days. My peak low score went up to 335 so I started running again, a mile slowly on a treadmill. Then the congestion came back fiercely. So I stopped all running and exercise and went back to Dr. Warner. I've got to give myself some credit here. I knew enough in 2015 to stop running when I wasn't feeling right. Back in 2012, I'd have continued to run, even with severe congestion. I hope I'm a little smarter now. Dr. Warner prescribed the appropriate medication. He also told me to up my Advair Diskus to twice a day and take ProAir as needed. (Richard Warner, MD, in discussion with the author, April 24, 2015).

I realized from this experience that I needed an Asthma Action Plan. This plan puts in writing the steps necessary to take when asthma symptoms get worse. On the next page is my personal Asthma Action Plan.

Asthma Action Plan

Date 7-12-15   Patient Name John Terry McConnell
Weight 152 lbs. Emergency Contact_____phone
Height 5'8"   Primary Care Provider Richard Warner, MD phone
Asthma triggers- pollen, mold, air pollution, dust, cold air, dairy products, stress, cigarette smoke
Baseline peak flow severity score 310
Best peak flow score 390
Medications
ProAir inhaler (albuterol sulfate) Inhalation Aerosol- two puffs before running
Advair Diskus 250/50 (fluticasone propionate 250 mcg and salmeterol 50 mcg inhalation powder) one inhalation upon waking up and another right before going to bed.
IC Montelukast SOD 10 mg tablet substituted for Singulair 10 mg tablet- 1 pill before bed
Green Zone- Breathing is good. Strenuous running or alternative exercise is done six days a week. Peak flow scores are between 325 and 390.
Yellow Zone- Chest congestion increases for one week. Running and alternative exercise is done less strenuously.

Drink a lot of decaf green tea. Peak flow scores are between 310 and 325. ProAir inhaler is taken as needed.

Red Zone- Dr. Warner is contacted and appointment to see him is made if increased chest congestion lasts for more than one week and/or peak flow scores are below 310. Drink a lot of decaf green tea. ProAir inhaler for quick relief is taken as needed. Running and alternative exercise ceases.

My Asthma Action Plan and my peak flow scores are valid only for me. By following it, I may avoid a serious illness in the future. You will have to determine how low your score gets before you stop running and contact your physician. The recommended guideline for determining your Green Zone is at least 80 percent of your best peak flow score; for the Yellow Zone it is between 50 and 80 percent of your best peak flow score, and for the Red Zone it is less than 50 percent. I suggest you write your own Asthma Action Plan with the help of your personal physician. ("Asthma Action Plan." Minnesota Department of Health. 2 Aug. 2013, http://www.health.state.mn.us/divs/hpcd/cdee/asthma/AAP-nonpro.html)

On April 25, 2015 a light bulb went on over my head. For years, I'd focused on using drugs like Advair Diskus and ProAir less. It had not occurred to me to use these drugs more when my congestion was severe. Now I know better. I can always cut back to the lower doses of these drugs when my chest congestion is less. I also realized that if I'd treated the bout of congestion I faced in the fall of 2012 the way I treated it in 2015, I might have been able to avoid that year's pneumonia. In late April 2015 my peak flow went back up to 360.

My running program began again in May 2015. My sights were set on a 5K race to take place in September, 2015. Late summer seems to be the time when my body works best. This race could be my shot at breaking twenty-six minutes for the 5K distance. In the summer of 2015 I noticed that my body was reacting differently to race preparation. In 2007 I raced best with a rest day two days before a race and a series of hundred meter hill sprints the day before the race. In 2014 I noticed I raced best with a rest day three days before a race, four hard four hundred meter runs two days before the race, and a swim the day before the race. Now, in 2015 I've been doing a time trial every three weeks. In my time trials this summer I've raced best with a hard run three days before the race, the Peaceful Warrior Workout and some upside down bicycle and V-up exercises two days before, and a rest day with only a four minute Peaceful Warrior Workout one day before the race. My race preparation is now quite different than it was in 2007. Why? Perhaps it is a change in my asthma. My chest congestion is less than it was in 2007. Now, if I don't exercise hard on a given day, I have very little congestion the next day. That's a huge change from 2007 when I had a lot of congestion every day. Perhaps my race preparation is now different because I'm eight years older. Perhaps it is because my workouts are now harder. Race preparation for optimum performance continues to be like a science experiment. I've discovered that my body has changed and now a rest day the day before the race works best. I think the lesson for me here is to continue to listen to my body and notice what race preparation works and what does not.

Here are two important ideas about running with asthma that I've learned (1) As I ramped up my running, I learned to take it slow. For me, over six decades of running, running hard has been risky. At times, running a hard workout or series of workouts resulted in illness for me. That's why the Immune System Daily Score Sheet is so important for me. Proper sleep, medications, diet, stress reduction, not increasing running mileage by more than 5 percent a week, and not running when feeling under par. These are my ways to protect myself from getting sick after a series of hard workouts. Sometimes illness is unavoidable but following the Immune System Daily Score Sheet lowers my odds of getting sick after a hard run. One solution to the problem of getting sick after running hard is to always run easy, just some easy jogging. But that's not me. I love to run hard.

Over the years, I've learned to walk a fine line. That line is between running too hard, too long and too easy, too short. For me, less is often more. Running too much weakens my immune system and leads to illness that prevents any running at all. That's why I run three days a week with an alternative exercise day after each running day. Then one day a week for rest.

(2) When I'm sick, I don't run or do any exercise. I let my body heal. Often when I'm not sick, I have congestion from an asthma trigger. For example, I just got back from a week of breathing the air in the Washington D.C. area. I was congested. After forty-five minutes of the Peaceful Warrior Workout and some other calisthenics, the congestion was gone. Slow jogging or other exercise like swimming or the Peaceful Warrior Workout helps relieve my congestion. When congested, hard, fast, vigorous running makes my congestion worse.

Running can be a powerful tool in improving your health and managing your asthma. Avoiding your asthma triggers; getting appropriate sleep, diet and stress reduction; knowing when running will improve your asthma and when it won't; knowing how much to run and how fast to run; these are the keys to running with asthma.

I still hope to break twenty-six minutes in my next 5K race. Regardless of that, running with asthma has given me priceless gifts- better breathing and better health.

I'd like to know about your experience running or playing sports with asthma. Please contact me with questions or comments at runnerwithasthma@gmail.com.

Bibliography

Adams, Abilgail. "Does Drinking Water Help Chest Congestion?" *LIVESTRONG.COM.*Last modified January 28, 2015. http://www.livestrong.com/article/480208-does-drinking-water-help-chest-congestion/.

Amacher, Walt. "Alberto Salazar: The Marathon Legend Talks about His Life." *On the Run Events.* Last modified 2000. http://www.ontherunevents.com/news/0264/.

"Applegate, Liz. "Nutrition Advice for Healthy, Hungry Runners." *Runner's World.* October 2013.

"Asthma." Paediatric Society of New Zealand and Starship Foundation. Last modified 2013. http://www.kidshealth.org.nz/asthma.

"Asthma." *The Free Dictionary.* Last modified February 8, 2015. http://medical-dictionary.thefreedictionary.com/Asthma.

"Asthma Action Plan." *Minnesota Department of Health.* August 2, 2013, http://www.health.state.mn.us/divs/hpcd/cdee/asthma/AAP-nonpro.html.

"Asthma All-Stars." *Breathe Easy Play Hard Foundation.* 2015. Last modified Feb. 4, 2015. http://www.breatheeasyplayhard.com/pg/jsp/general/asthmaallstars.jsp#olympic.

"Asthma and Colds: Symptoms, Causes, Bacterial Infections, and More." *WebMD.* Last modified 2011. http://www.webmd.com/cold-and-flu/cold-guide/asthma_colds.

"Asthma Health Center Exercise and Asthma." *WebMD*. Last modified 2010. http://www.webmd.com/asthma/guide/exercising-asthma.

"Asthma and the Peak Flow Meter." *WebMD*. Last modified 2013. http://www.webmd.com/asthma/guide/peak-flow-meter.

"Asthma: Personal Stories—Former US Rep. Jim Ryun." Asthma Care Guide. *PennMedicine*. Last modified 2011. http://www.pennmedicine.org/health_info/asthma/000124.html.

"Asthma Statistics." *American Academy of Allergy, Asthma and Immunology*. Last modified 2014. http://www.aaaai.org/about-the-aaaai/newsroom/asthma-statistics.aspx.

"The Athlete's Guide to Exercise-Induced Asthma." *WebMD*. Last modified 2011. http://www.webmd.boots.com/asthma/guide/athletes-guide-exercise-induced-asthma?page=2.

Babb, Diane. "Asthma—Run with It!" *Road Runner Sports*. Last modified May 26, 2014. http://www.roadrunnersports.com/rrs/content/content.jsp?contentId=300078.

Bass, Pat. "Diet and Asthma: Are My Diet and Asthma Symptoms Related?" *About.com*. Last modified June 6, 2010. http://asthma.about.com/od/asthmacam/a/asthma_diet.htm.

"Benefits of Learning Tai Chi." *Energy Arts*. Last modified 2013. http://www.energyarts.com/benefits-learning-tai-chi.

Binder, Doug. "Mo Farah, Galen Rupp, Kara Goucher Shine at New York Half Marathon."*OregonLive*.com. Last modified March 21, 2011. http://www.oregonlive.com/trackandfield/index.ssf/2011/03/mo_farah_galen_rupp_kara_gouch.html.

Bowden, Jonny. *The 150 Healthiest Foods on Earth: The Surprising, Unbiased Truth about What You Should Eat and Why.* Gloucester, MA: Fair Winds, 2007.

Brant, John. "Frank's Story." *Runner's World.* October 2011.

"Breathe Easier: Have Asthma? Running in the Morning May Help." *Runner's World.* March 2003.

Broadbent, Rick. "Haile Gebrselassie's Story Set to Run and Run." *Sunday Times.* January 19, 2009. http://www.timesonline.co.uk/tol/sport/olympics/article5542399.ece.

Brook, U., and I. Tepper. "Self Image, Coping and Familial Interaction among Asthmatic Children and Adolescents in Israel." *Patient Education and Counseling: An International Journal for Communication and Healthcare.* February 1997. http://www.ncbi.nlm.nih.gov/pubmed/9128620.

Brostoff, Jonathan, and Linda Gamlin. *Asthma: The Complete Guide to Integrative Therapies.* Rochester, VT: Healing Arts Press, 2000.

Burfoot, Amby. *Runner's World Complete Book of Running: Everything You Need to Know to Run for Fun, Fitness, and Competition.* Emmaus, PA: Rodale, 1997.

"CDC Vital Signs—Asthma in the US." *Centers for Disease Control and Prevention.* Last modified May 4, 2011. http://www.cdc.gov/VitalSigns/Asthma/index.html.

Cheng, Maria. "Study: More than 600,000 People Killed by 2nd-Hand Smoke." *Greenfield Recorder.* November 26, 2010.

Couzens, Gerald S. "Breathtaking Workouts." *Women's Sports and Fitness.* September 1991.

Dean, Carolyn. "Effect of Oral Magnesium Supplementation on Asthma." *Natural Medicine Journal.* May 2010. http://naturalmedicinejournal.com/journal/2010-05/effect-oral-magnesium-supplementation-asthma.

"Dehydration Makes Exercise-Induced Asthma Worse, Study by UB Researchers Finds." *ScienceDaily.* June 7, 1999. http://www.sciencedaily.com/releases/1999/06/990607071643.htm.

Doheny, Kathleen. "Too Much Running Tied to Shorter Life Span." *WebMD.* Last modified April 1, 2014. http://www.webmd.com/fitness-exercise/20140401/too-much-running-tied-to-shorter-lifespan-studies-find.

Dreyer, Danny, and Katherine Dreyer. *Chi Running: A Revolutionary Approach to Effortless, Injury-Free Running.* New York: Simon and Schuster, 2009.

"Exercise and Asthma." *WebMD.* Last modified 2015. http://www.webmd.com/asthma/guide/exercising-asthma.

"Exercise and Immunity." *MedicinePlus.* National Institutes of Health, US National Library of Medicine. Last modified May 15, 2012. http://www.nlm.nih.gov/medlineplus/ency/article/007165.htm.

"Exercise-Induced Asthma." *WebMD.* Last modified April 16, 2010. http://www.emedicinehealth.com/exercise-induced_asthma/article_em.htm.

"Exercise-Induced Asthma Common among Olympic Athletes." *Medical News Today: Health News*. 2011. http://www.medicalnews-today.com/articles/37004.php.

Fitzgerald, Matt. "Rupp Kicks His Way to a Third 10,000m title." *Competitor Network*. June 24, 2011. http://running.competitor.com/2011/06/news/rupp-kicks-way-to-a-third-10000m-title_30603.

Fried, Robert. *Breathe Well, Be Well: A Program to Relieve Stress, Anxiety, Asthma, Hypertension, Migraine, and Other Disorders for Better Health*. Hoboken, NJ: Wiley, 1999.

"Galen Rupp Steps off Track in Boise." *Track Focus*. January 23, 2011. http://www.trackfocus.com/gprofile.php?mgroup_id=45597&do=news&news_id= 213325.

Girdwain, Jessica. "Arms Race." *Runner's World*. December 2013.

Griffin, R. Morgan. "Asthma and Cities: Which Cities Rank Best?" *WebMD*. Last modified 2011. http://www.webmd.com/asthma/features/asthma-and-cities-which-cities-ran-best?page=3.

Hall, John R. "Watch Out for Indoor Pollutants." *Air Conditioning, Heating and Refrigeration News*. December 22, 2003.

"Hall of Fame." *USA Track & Field*. Last modified 2011. http://www.usatf.org/halloffame/TF/showBio.asp?HOFIDs=196.

Hamilton, Tish. "Your Friend, Kara! (Inc.)." *Runner's World*. November 2014.

Hebert, Dean. "The Running World According to Dean." Last modified May 2, 2009. http://coachdeanhebert.wordpress.com/author/coachdeanhebert/page/15/.

Hendrick, Bill. "Asthma Rates on Rise in US." *WebMD*. Last modified May 3, 2011. http://www.webmd.com/asthma/news/20110503/asthma-rates-on-the-rise-in-the-us.

Hendrick, Bill. "Tai Chi May Help Control Asthma." *WebMD*. Last modified October 29, 2008. http://www.webmd.com/asthma/news/20081028/tai-chi-may-help-control-asthma.

"High Rate of Asthma Found in College Athletes." *Science Daily*. September 9, 2007. http://www.sciencedaily.com/releases/2007/09/070905080810.htm.

Hogshead, Nancy, and Gerald S. Couzens. *Asthma and Exercise*. New York: Henry Holt and Company, 1990.

"How Paula Overcame Asthma." *BBC News*. Last modified June 4, 2011. http://news.bbc.co.uk/sportacademy/hi/sa/treatment_room/features/newsid_2346000/2346883.stm.

"How Stress Causes Asthma Complications." *WebMD*. Last modified 2010. http://www.webmd.com/asthma/guide/stress-asthma.

Howden-Chapman, Phillippa. "Effects of Improved Home Heating on Asthma in Community Dwelling Children: Randomized Controlled Trial." *BMJ*. September 23, 2008. http://www.bmj.com/content/337/bmj.a1411.

Howe, Peter J. "Roxbury Students March against Pollution." *Boston Globe*, October 23, 1997.

Hutchinson, Alex. "The 'Asthmatic Advantage' at the Olympics." *Runner's World*. Last modified July 30, 2012. http://www.runnersworld.com/health/asthmatic-advantage-olympics.

Jhung, Lisa. "The New Core Curriculum." *Runner's World*, February 2014.

Kalhoff, H. "Mild Dehydration: A Risk Factor of Broncho-Pulmonary Disorders." *European Journal of Clinical Nutrition* 57.S2 (2003): S81.

Kallstrom, Thomas J. "Smoking and the Asthma Patient." *Allergy and Asthma Health*. American Association of Respiratory Care (Summer 2007). http://www.yourlunghealth.org/healthy_living/aah/07.07/articles/smoking.

Kardong, Don. "Bright Speed." *Runner's World*, July 1997.

King, Stephen. *On Writing: A Memoir of the Craft*. New York: Scribner, 2000.

Knight, Tom. "Haile Gebrselassie on Brink of Olympic U-turn." *Telegraph*. March 11, 2008. http://www.telegraph.co.uk/sport/othersports/olympics/2294156/Haile-Gebrselassie-on-brink-of-Olympic-U-turn.html.

Lam, Paul. "Tai Chi for Arthritis." *Arthritis Foundation*. 2009 DVD.

Levine, Barbara Hoberman. *Your Body Believes Every Word You Say*. Fairfield, CT: WordsWork, 2000.

Li, James T. MD, PhD. "My daughter has asthma. Should we replace the carpeting in our home with wood flooring?" *Mayo Clinic*. Last modified April 30, 2013. http://www.mayoclinic.org/diseases-conditions/childhood-asthma/expert-answers/asthma-triggers/faq-20057785.

Lorge Butler, Sarah. "Don't Stop Now." *Runner's World*. July 2010.

McDougall, Christopher. *Born to Run: A Hidden Tribe, Superathletes, and the Greatest Race the World Has Never Seen*. New York: Alfred A. Knopf, 2010.

McMillan, Greg. "Change Your Ways." *Runner's World*. January 2006.

"Marathon Records." *MarathonGuide.com*. Last modified 4 June 4, 2011. http://www.marathonguide.com/history/records/all-timelist.cfm?Gen=F.

Mayo Clinic Staff. "Asthma: Causes." *Mayo Clinic*. Last modified 2011. http://www.mayoclinic.com/health/asthma/DS00021/DSECTION=causes.

Mayo Clinic Staff. "Asthma: Definition." *Mayo Clinic*. Last modified 2011. http://www.mayoclinic.com/health/asthma/DS00021.

Mayo Clinic Staff. "Water: How Much Should You Drink Every Day?" *Mayo Clinic*. Last modified August 2, 2011. http://www.mayoclinic.com/health/water/NU00283.

"Medication Guide—Advair Diskus." Research Triangle Park, NC: GlaxoSmithKline, 2010.

"Mental Stress, Physical Illness." *WebMD*. Last modified 2002. http://www.webmd.com/mental-health/news/20020812/mental-stress-physical-illness.

Munson, Marty. "Shooting the Wheeze: Continuous Warm-Up May Keep Asthma Away." *Prevention*. January 1995.

"Nebulizers: Home and Portable." *WebMD*. Last modified 2014. http://www.webmd.com/asthma/guide/home-nebulizer-therapy?print=true.

"New Research on Asthma from University of Victoria Summarized." *Women's Health Weekly*. March 25, 2010.

Page, Linda, and Sarah Abernathy. *Healthy Healing*. 14th Edition. Eden Prairie, MN: Healthy Healing Publications, 2011.

Parsons, Jonathon P., Teal S. Hallstrand, John G. Mastronarde, David A. Kaminsky, Kenneth W. Rundell, James H. Hull, William W. Storms, John M. Weiler, Fern M. Cheek, Kevin C. Wilson, and Sandra D Anderson. "An Official American Thoracic Society Clinical Practice Guideline: Exercise-Induced Bronchoconstriction." *American Thoracic Society*. 2013.

PROAIR HFA (Albuterol Sulfate) Inhalation Aerosol. Waterford, Ireland: IVAX Pharmaceuticals, 2010.

Pruitt, Bill. "The Struggle to Breathe...When Asthma Attacks Sleep." *Sleep Review* (March 2009). http://galesites.com/menu/mlin_w_arms.

"Psychological Issues Plague Patients with Asthma." *Clinical Advisor* (2010).

Richards, Warren. "Preventing Behavior Problems in Asthma and Allergies." *Clinical Pediatrics* 33.10 (1994): 617. http://galesites.com/menu/mlin_w_arms.

Rieves, D. "Suffer the Children." *Chest* (2002): 394-96.

Rinkunas, Susan. "6 Tips for Running with Asthma." *Women's Health.* Last modified March 22, 2013. http://www.womenshealthmag.com/fitness/running-asthma.

Ritchison, Gary. "Lecture Notes 6—Respiratory System Bio 301 Human Physiology." *Eastern Kentucky University.* Last modified 2011. http://people.eku.edu/ritchisong/301syl.html.

Rosenbaum, Mike. "Haile Gebrselassie: Double-Gold Medalist at 10,000 Meters." *About.com.* Last modified 2011. http://trackand-field.about.com/od/longdistance/p/profilegebrsela.htm.

"Running with Asthma: Breathe Easy." *Men's Health.* Last modified February 25, 2004. http://www.menshealth.com/health/running-asthma.

Salazar, Alberto and Rick Lovett. *Alberto Salazar's Guide to Running.* Camden, ME: Ragged Mountain Press, 2001.

Schaeffer, Janis. "Beph.com: Asthma All-Stars." *BreatheEasyPlayHard.com.* Last modified 2010. http://www.breatheeasyplayhard.com/pg/jsp/general/asthmaallstars.jsp.

Schiro, Tara. "If You're Running with Asthma You Must Run Consistently." *TaraSchiro.WordPress.com.* Last modified August 2011. http://taraschiro.wordpress.com/2011/08/13/if-youre-running-with-asthma-you-must-run-consistently/.

Schiro, Tara. "Asthma 'Cured' with Long Distance Running." *TaraSchiro.WordPress.com.* Last modified October 6, 2009. http://taraschiro.wordpress.com/2009/10/06/asthma-cured-with-long-distance-running/.

Schrock, Susan. "Breathing New Life." *Greenfield Recorder.* August 20, 2013.

Schroeder, Stephanie. "Let's Try Heavy Breath: Doing It Right Feels a Little Different (I Tried It)." *Curve.* May 2007.

"Statistics." *American Academy of Allergy, Asthma and Immunology.* Last modified 2011. http://www.aaaai.org/media/statistics/asthma-statistics.asp.

"Stress and Asthma." *WebMD.* Last modified 2014. http://www.webmd.com/asthma/guide/stress-asthma?page=3.

"Swimming with Asthma." *University of Tasmania.* Last modified May 10, 2013. http://www.sciencealert.com.au/news/20131005-24359.html.

Traister, Jeffery. "The Benefits of Fruit and Vegetables for Asthma." *WebMD.*Last modified December 5, 2010. http://www.livestrong.com/article/325717-the-benefits-of-fruits-vegetables-for-asthma/.

"Tree-Lined Streets Mean Lower Rates of Childhood Asthma, Study Suggests." *Science Daily,* April 30, 2008. http://www.sciencedaily.com/releases/2008/04/080430201651.htm.

Warner, Jennifer. "Watching Salt Intake Won't Help Asthma." *WebMD.* Last modified July 15, 2008. http://www.webmd.com/asthma/news/20080715/watching-salt-intake-wont-shake-asthma.

Zand, Janet, Allan Spreen, and James LaValle. *Smart Medicine for Healthier Living: A Practical A-to-Z Reference to Natural and Conventional Treatments for Adults.* New York: Avery Publishing Group, 1999.

Index

Printed in Great Britain
by Amazon

33066033R00066